UNDP/UNCHS/World Bank
Urban Management Programme

W0037715

Urban Management and the Environment

14

Rapid Urban Environmental Assessment

Lessons from Cities in the Developing World
Volume 1. Methodology and Preliminary Findings

Josef Leitmann

Published for the Urban Management Programme by
The World Bank, Washington, D.C.

This document has been prepared under the auspices of the United Nations Development Programme/United Nations Centre for Human Settlements (Habitat)/World Bank–sponsored Urban Management Programme. The findings, interpretations, and conclusions expressed here are those of the authors and do not necessarily represent the views of the United Nations Development Programme, UNCHS, the World Bank, or any of their affiliated organizations.

Deputy Director
Division for Global
  and Interregional Programmes
United Nations Development
  Programme
	Chief
	Technical Co-operation
	  Division
	United Nations Centre
	  for Human Settlements
	  (Habitat)
		Chief
		Urban Development Division
		Transport, Water, and Urban
		  Development Department
		Environmentally Sustainable
		  Development

Copyright © 1994
The International Bank for Reconstruction
and Development/THE WORLD BANK
1818 H Street, N.W.
Washington, D.C. 20433, U.S.A.

All rights reserved
Manufactured in the United States of America
First printing May 1994
Second printing February 1995

The Urban Management Programme (UMP) represents a major approach by the United Nations family of organizations, together with external support agencies (ESAS), to strengthen the contribution that cities and towns in developing countries make toward economic growth, social development, and the alleviation of poverty. The program seeks to develop and promote appropriate policies and tools for municipal finance and administration, land management, infrastructure management, environmental management, and poverty alleviation. Through a capacity building component, the UMP plans to establish an effective partnership with national, regional, and global networks and ESAS in applied research, dissemination of information, and experiences of best practices and promising options.

The findings, interpretations, and conclusions expressed in this paper are entirely those of the author(s) and should not be attributed in any manner to the World Bank, to its affiliated organizations, or to members of its Board of Executive Directors or the countries they represent. The World Bank does not guarantee the accuracy of the data included in this publication and accepts no responsibility whatsoever for any consequence of their use. Some sources cited in this paper may be informal documents that are not readily available. The boundaries, colors, denominations, and other information shown on any map in this volume do not imply on the part of the World Bank Group any judgment on the legal status of any territory or the endorsement or acceptance of such boundaries.

The material in this publication is copyrighted. Requests for permission to reproduce portions of it should be sent to the Office of the Publisher at the address shown in the copyright notice above. The World Bank encourages dissemination of its work and will normally give permission promptly and, when the reproduction is for noncommercial purposes, without asking a fee. Permission to copy portions for classroom use is granted through the Copyright Clearance Center, Inc., Suite 910, 222 Rosewood Drive, Danvers, Massachusetts 01923, U.S.A.

ISSN: 1020-0215

Library of Congress Cataloging-in-Publication Data

Leitmann, Josef.
    Rapid urban environmental assessment : lessons from cities in the
developing world / Josef Leitmann.
       p.   cm. — (Urban management and the environment, ISSN
  1020-0215 ; 14)
    Includes bibliographical references.
    Contents: v. 1. Methodology and preliminary findings.
    ISBN 0-8213-2790-9
    1. Urban management program. 2. Cities and towns—Developing
countries—Environmental conditions. 3. Environmental risk
assessment—Developing countries. 4. Urban ecology—Developing
countries. 5. Environmental policy—Developing countries.
I. UNDP/UNCHS/World Bank Urban Management Programme. II. Title.
III. Series: Urban management program. Urban management and the
environment ; 14.
GE160.D44L45   1994
363.7'009173'2—dc20
                                     94-10848
                                      CIP

CONTENTS

FIGURE

BOXES

FOREWORD

This paper has been prepared for the environment component of the Urban Management Programme (UMP), a joint undertaking of the United Nations Development Programme (UNDP), the United Nations Centre for Human Settlements (UNCHS), and the World Bank. The UMP represents a major cooperative and coordinated effort by the United Nations family of organizations, together with external support agencies, to strengthen the contribution that cities and towns in developing countries make toward economic growth, social development, and the alleviation of poverty. The UMP develops and promotes appropriate policies and tools for urban environmental management, infrastructure, land management, urban poverty alleviation, and municipal finance and administration. Through capacity building, the UMP is establishing an effective partnership with national, regional, and global networks and ESAs (external support agencies) in applied research, information dissemination, and exchanges of experience concerning best practices and options.

A milestone was achieved at the UNCED Earth Summit (Rio de Janeiro, 1992) when cities were successful in broadening the environmental debate to focus attention on urban priorities. There was broad-based agreement that the developing world's growing urban populations need attention, and their main concern is the "brown agenda"—involving pollution problems, environmental hazards, and poverty. The Earth Summit also recognized that local authorities and interest groups are best able to take concrete actions on the urban environment. The challenge now is to maintain the momentum built up before and during the summit and to implement the decisions reached at UNCED.

A second milestone occurred at the final meeting of the Ford Foundation-supported global review of urban research in the developing world (Cairo, 1993). Although virtually every regional analysis in this two-year study emphasized the urban environment as a priority topic for the urban research agenda in the 1990s, there was scant evidence of actual research having been completed and disseminated. During the last decade, explicit research on the urban environment only constituted between 1.5% (Southern Africa) and 4% (southern cone of Latin America) of the urban research portfolio.

The consequence of these milestones is a need for action at the local level. Yet there is little solid information available for planning and making decisions. One solution for resolving this contradiction is to apply the methodology for rapid urban environmental assessment that is developed in this paper. The methodology has been explicitly designed to be low cost, rapid, locally managed, and participatory. The first volume in this set presents the techniques, derives general lessons for urban environmental management from their application in a select number of cities, and suggests future directions and improvements. The second volume consists of the tools that make up the methodology and summaries of information that they generated.

Phase 2 of the UMP (1992-96) is concerned with capacity building at both the country and regional levels and with facilitating national and municipal dialogue on policy and program options. It emphasizes a participatory structure that draws on the strengths of developing country experts and expedites the dissemination of that expertise at the local, national, regional, and global levels.

Through its regional offices in Africa, the Arab States, Asia and the Pacific, and Latin America and the Caribbean, the UMP seeks to strengthen urban management by harnessing the skills and strategies of regional experts, communities, and organizations in the private sector.

Regional coordinators use these networks to address the five programme themes in two ways:

- **City and country consultations.** The UMP brings together national and local authorities, private-sector networks, community representatives, and other actors to discuss specific problems within the UMP's subject areas and to propose reasoned solutions. Consultations are held at the request of a country or city, and often provide a forum for discussion of a cross-section of issues.

- **Technical cooperation.** To sustain follow-up to the consultations, the UMP uses its regional networks of expertise to provide technical advice and cooperation.

Through its nucleus team in Nairobi and Washington, DC, the UMP supports its regional programmes and networks by synthesizing lessons learned, conducting state-of-the-art research, and supporting dissemination of programme related materials.

Mark Hildebrand
Chief
Technical Cooperation Division
United Nations Centre for
Human Settlements (HABITAT)

Louis Y. Pouliquen
Director
Transportation, Water, and
Urban Development Department

ABSTRACT

The 1992 UNCED Earth Summit concluded that the environmental problems of the world's growing urban population need attention; however, the 1993 Ford Foundation-supported evaluation of urban research in developing countries noted that scant data are available on the urban environment, as little research has been done on this topic. Thus, there is a need for environmental action at the local level, but there is little solid information available for building public commitment, planning, and decision making. One solution for resolving this contradiction is to apply the methodology for rapid urban environmental assessment that is developed in this report. The methodology has been explicitly designed to be low cost, rapid, locally managed, and participatory; it is also a possible starting point for environmental planning and management.

The first volume in this set is designed for an audience of urban managers, policy makers, analysts, and researchers. It presents the techniques, summarizes results from applying the approach in a select number of cities, and suggests future directions and improvements. The first chapter provides information on the development of the methodology; preliminary findings and future directions for research are offered in the second chapter; and comparative results from the assessments are summarized in Annex III. The second volume is composed of the tools that can be directly applied in the field by practitioners and researchers. It consists of the questionnaire, generic profile and consultation guidelines that make up the methodology, and summaries of the information that they generated.

ACKNOWLEDGMENTS

This paper was written by Josef Leitmann of the World Bank's Urban Development Division, who also directed the field research. The work could not have been done without the knowledge, experience, and specialized skills of key local consultants in the seven case study cities on four continents, listed in Annex 1. Thanks are also due to numerous individuals who have commented on earlier versions of this work: Patricia Annez, Carl Bartone, Jochen Eigen, Anna Haines, Richard Meier, Robert Twiss, Melvin Webber, and David Williams. Excellent contributions were also made by the external reviewers of this publication: Adrian Atkinson (Coordinator, GTZ Urban Environmental Guidelines Project), Carlos Linares (Associate, World Resources Institute), Gordon McGranahan (Senior Research Fellow, Stockholm Environment Institute), and Manida Unkulvasapaul (Water and Sanitation Consultant, Bangkok).

ABBREVIATIONS

AMA	Accra Metropolitan Authority
BOD	biochemical oxygen demand
DKI	National Capital Area (of Jakarta)
EAP	environmental action plan
EIA	environmental impact assessment
EMS	environmental management strategy
EPA	US Environmental Protection Agency
ICLEI	International Council for Local Environmental Initiatives
IULA	International Union of Local Authorities
Jabotabek	Jakarta metropolitan region
OECD	Organization for Economic Cooperation and Development
SEI	Stockholm Environment Institute
SCP	UNCHS (Habitat) Sustainable Cities Programme
SWM	solid waste management
TMG	Tianjin Municipal Government
UMP	UNDP/UNCHS (Habitat)/World Bank Urban Management Programme
UMP/E	Environment component of the UMP
UNCHS	United Nations Centre for Human Settlements
UNDP	United Nations Development Programme
UNEP	United Nations Environmental Programme
USAID	US Agency for International Development

EXECUTIVE SUMMARY

i.   The 1992 UNCED Earth Summit concluded that the environmental problems of the world's growing urban population need attention; however, the 1993 Ford Foundation-supported evaluation of urban research in developing countries noted that scant data are available on the urban environment, as little research has been done on this topic. Thus, there is a need for environmental action at the local level, but there is little solid information available for building public commitment, planning, and decision making. One solution for resolving this contradiction is to apply the methodology for rapid urban environmental assessment that is developed in this report. The methodology has been explicitly designed to be low cost, rapid, locally managed, and participatory; it is also a possible starting point for environmental planning and management.

ii.   **Who is the audience for this publication? How is it organized?** The first volume in this set is designed for an audience of urban managers, policy makers, analysts, and researchers. It presents the techniques, summarizes results from applying the approach in a select number of cities, and suggests future directions and improvements. The first chapter provides information on the development of the methodology; preliminary findings and future directions for research are offered in the second chapter; and comparative results from the assessments are summarized in Annex III. The second volume is composed of the tools that can be directly applied in the field by practitioners and researchers. It consists of the questionnaire, generic profile and consultation guidelines that make up the methodology, and summaries of the information that they generated.

Background

iii.   The rapid urban environmental assessment approach was developed by the environment component of the Urban Management Programme (UMP), a joint undertaking of the United Nations Development Programme, the United Nations Centre for Human Settlements (UNCHS-Habitat), and the World Bank. This activity had two objectives: to address gaps in knowledge and to test a process that can support efforts to manage the urban environment. Very little information is readily available on environmental conditions, the interaction between urban development and ecosystems, or the managerial setting that exists to respond to environmental problems in the cities of the developing world. Recent attempts to develop such information have been incomplete. Thus, there appears to be a need for urban environmental research that is comprehensive, multisectoral, relatively short term, and consistent between cities. Similarly, there is a need for an informed, action-oriented process that can support better environmental planning and management at the city level. Any methodology that meets these objectives must face a more important test: relevance and utility in a diversity of cities.

Methodology

iv.   In the same spirit as rapid and participatory rural appraisal, a three-step process was developed to rapidly assess the state of the urban environment:

> • An **urban environmental data questionnaire** was designed to measure a consistent set of data that are cross-sectoral and cross-media in nature.

- An **urban environmental profile** was outlined to analyze the nature, trends, and factors that influence environmental quality in cities.

- The framework of a **consultation process** was developed to initiate a public dialogue on environmental priorities and options as well as to partially validate the results of the questionnaire and profile through public discussion.

The tools that constitute each of these three steps and sample results from their application are presented in Volume 2.

v.　　Rapid assessment can be the first step in a strategic approach to urban environmental planning and management. The technique helps to clarify issues, involve key actors, identify priorities, and build political commitment in a setting where some or all of these elements are lacking. Subsequent steps in the strategic approach are: (a) the formulation of an integrated **urban environmental management strategy** that embodies issue-specific strategies, long-term environmental goals, and phased targets for meeting the goals; (b) agreement on **issues-oriented action plans** for achieving the targets, including identification of least-cost project options, policy reforms, and institutional actions; and (c) a **consolidation** phase where agreed programs and projects are initiated, policy reforms and institutional arrangements are solidified, the overall process is made routine, and monitoring and evaluation procedures are put in place. More information on this strategic approach can be found in *Towards Environmental Strategies for Cities*, Urban Management Programme Discussion Paper (forthcoming).

vi.　　The case study approach was selected to test the methodology because it is a valid research tool in the absence of theoretical guidance in this field. The following criteria were used to select the cases: (a) the cities should be chosen from different continents, cultures, and political systems; (b) they should reflect different levels of per capita income, with varying degrees of poverty; (c) they should be characterized by different stages and types of industrialization; (d) both large and small cities should be included in the sample; and (e) baseline data should be available from ongoing activities so that primary research can be minimized. These criteria were combined with a resource constraint to select six cities and one urbanizing area: Accra (Ghana), Jakarta (Indonesia), Katowice (Poland), São Paulo (Brazil), Tianjin (China), Tunis (Tunisia), and the Singrauli region (India).

vii.　　After applying the technique in these cities, several lessons were learned about its strengths and limitations, as well as areas for further inquiry. The advantages of the rapid assessment methodology are that it: (a) is indeed rapid; (b) costs relatively little to use; (c) centralizes diverse information; and (d) benefits from local knowledge, access to, and discussion of information. Taken in isolation from the other phases in the strategic approach to environmental management, the technique suffers from three limitations: (a) it provides guidance as to what might be a priority problem but gives little indication as to what might constitute the range of possible solutions; (b) by using secondary data, it is confined by the range and quality of work that has already been done; and (c) results cannot always be compared between cities because data apply to different time periods, were derived in different ways, or are based on a different sample. The first drawback can be overcome when the methodology is linked to a strategic approach for urban environmental management. The second problem can be addressed by identifying and following up on areas that would benefit from new or improved research. The third issue is a problem for cross-urban analysis but not for environmental problem solving in a single city.

viii.   Some topics that would constitute fruitful areas for future research include: gathering data on low-income communities; linking health effects with environmental conditions; valuing the economic costs and benefits of urban environmental activities; using alternative methods to assess public priorities; matching jurisdictions with ecological boundaries; and comparing policy instruments for environmental management. New research has already been initiated on some of these topics. As new knowledge is developed from this research and from increasing use of the rapid-assessment methodology, the approach will be refined and modified to better serve as an initial instrument for managing environmental quality in cities of the developing world.

Tentative Conclusions for Urban Environmental Management

ix.   Initial results from the rapid assessments have yielded three sets of preliminary findings. In the area of urban poverty and economic structure, it appears that:

- **Urban environmental degradation has a disproportionate negative impact on the poor**. The poor suffer disproportionately from urban environmental insults; environmentally sensitive and hazardous urban areas are often inhabited by the poor; the poor pay more for basic environmental services and infrastructure; income is not always the best measure of poor quality of life; and targeted interventions can improve the environmental conditions of low-income groups.

- **Economic structure shapes environmental problems**. The structure and location of economic activities in and around cities affect the prevalence and severity of particular environmental problems. The important economic variables that appear to influence environmental problems are: spatial patterns of industrial location and impacts on health; the effectiveness of industrial pollution control; energy use and industrial structure; and the size and nature of the informal sector.

- **The level of urban wealth is linked to certain environmental problems**. Basic sanitation is a problem of low-income cities. Hazardous wastes, ambient air pollution, and lack of green space are priority problems of higher-incomes cities. Surface water pollution and inadequate solid waste management are problems that plague developing urban areas, regardless of their level of wealth.

x.   In the area of urban institutions and management, the following is suggested from the results of the rapid urban environmental assessments:

- **Environmental management is complex**. Managing urban environmental problems is complicated because of the following: the large number of actors per problem area; cross-jurisdictional conflicts; central-local conflicts; and tension between forces for centralization and devolution of authority.

- **Institutions, policies, and problems are not synchronized**. Part of the managerial complexity stems from the fact that there is often little relationship between the spatial scale or nature of urban environmental problems, which are often cross-sectoral, and the design of sectoral institutions and policies.

4

- **Municipal capacity affects environmental quality.** If solutions to particular environmental problems are within the purview of municipal institutions, they must have appropriate financial and human resources. When resources are inadequate, the maintenance and/or expansion of environmental services and infrastructure will be constrained.

xi.   In the area of problem analysis and prioritization, preliminary conclusions indicate that:

- **Public opinion and professional/scientific priorities may differ.** Neither public opinion nor scientific analysis provides the optimal means of ranking urban environmental problems; both the public and the analytic processes have their biases; and a combined approach offers the potential for improving each process.

- **Cities have significant extra-urban environmental impacts.** Urban demand for resources and the disposal of city wastes that result from resource transformation can harm environmental systems outside the city proper.

xii.   These findings offer potentially useful advice for those seeking to improve environmental management in Third World cities. The following general conclusions flow from these tentative results of the assessment exercise: (a) urban environmental strategies should have an explicit focus on the problems of the poor; (b) city-specific strategies should be guided by the configuration of key economic variables; (c) solutions that are not heavily dependent on institutional performance may be necessary in the short run because of the organizational problems of complexity and synchronization; (d) enhanced public awareness, consultation, and participation can improve environmental management; and (e) careful attention must be paid to the selection of problem areas, their scale, and institutional capacity when designing interventions.

Synthesis of Substantive Results

xiii.   Annex III summarizes a wealth of substantive results from the case study cities that were generated by the rapid assessments, particularly the questionnaires and profiles. Preliminary findings are presented on:

- The **status of the environment in the urban region**—the quality of environmental systems (air, water, land); environmental hazards.

- The **interaction between urban development and the environment**—how environmental factors shape urban development; the impact of urban development on the immediate environment (population growth, family planning, water supply and distribution, sanitation, municipal and industrial waste disposal, urban energy consumption, transportation and telecommunications, housing, mining, health and health care systems); the impact of urban development on rural areas.

- The **institutional setting for environmental management**—key actors; management functions (instruments, coordination and decision-making); constraints and opportunities.

xiv.   No attempt is made to present more detailed information in this executive summary because the contents of Annex III already represent a summary of the case study findings. Finally, a matrix is used to present a compendium of urban environmental issues and options; it classifies problem areas by medium (air, water, land, and cross-media) and summarizes their effects, causes, and management options.

I. INTRODUCTION TO THE ASSESSMENT METHODOLOGY

This chapter describes the rapid urban environmental assessment methodology developed by the Urban Management and the Environment Program (UMP/E). To begin, the objectives of the UMP/E and the role of research within the program are briefly described. Then, there is a selective review of recent efforts in the area of urban environmental assessment; the limitations of this body of work help to identify needed improvements on previous research efforts, as well as overall objectives for the research. Next, the assessment approach is presented. The methodology consists of a three-step process:

1) completion of a questionnaire on urban environmental data;

2) preparation of an urban environmental profile, using data from the question- naire and research assistance from local investigators; and

3) discussion of the results through a series of consultations, culminating in a priority-focused public workshop.

This technique was tested in seven cases globally. Criteria are presented for selecting the sites and methodological lessons from the case studies are reviewed. In addition to yielding research results, the assessment process can support a strategic approach to urban management that includes preparation of investments and the development of policy changes for improving urban environmental quality.

Urban Management and the Environment

1.1   The rapid urban environmental assessment approach has been developed by the Urban Management and Environment component of the joint UNDP/UNCHS (Habitat)/World Bank Urban Management Programme (UMP). The background material for this report has been used, in combination with discussion papers and research, to develop an overall document on **environmental strategies for cities**.[1] The profiles and environmental data served as inputs for, *inter alia*, interna- tional forums on cities and the environment, the UNCHS Sustainable Cities Programme, the World Bank's *World Development Report 1992*, and the preparation of urban environmental projects. In turn, the results of these and other activities will be used to improve the assessment process over time.

1.2   In addition to city-based activities, the environmental component of the UMP is preparing background papers and undertaking research. Background papers cover urban waste management and pollution control, energy-environment linkages in the urban sector, regulatory and economic instruments for pollution control, the environmental dimensions of urban land use, and the urban environmental planning and management process. Each is designed to provide background information on key urban development-environment linkages and/or suggest elements of an environmental-management strategy for cities in the developing world. Reports have been prepared and research is continuing on: (a) the health impacts of urban environmental problems; (b) the economic valuation of urban environmental problems; (c) urban environmental data collection;

---

1. See *Toward Environmental Strategies for Cities: Policy Considerations for Urban Environmental Management in Developing Countries* (forthcoming), UMP Discussion Paper, Washington, DC: World Bank, 1993.

(d) the local management of hazardous wastes from small-scale and cottage industries; and (e) the application of remote sensing and geographic information systems to urban environmental planning. Finally, new work is commencing on the economics and finance of urban waste management, urban environmental data collection at the household level, urban air pollution-control strategies, and evaluation of private sector delivery of solid waste services.

Guidance from the Recent Past: Obstacles and Objectives

1.3 Little information is readily available on environmental conditions, the interaction between urban development and ecosystems, or the managerial setting that exists to respond to environmental problems in the cities of the developing world.[2] Recent attempts to develop such information have been incomplete because they: (a) focused on a limited number of variables that do not present a complete picture of key environmental issues in metropoloi[3]; (b) took a narrow perspective by examining only one sector within the city[4]; (c) required several years of intensive, multidisciplinary research and analysis[5]; or (d) did not develop a set of urban environmental data that would allow for comparison across different types of cities[6]. The end result is that much of this work has not been immediately relevant to those who must respond to the environmental consequences of

---

2. The Ford Foundation-supported global review of urban research in the developing world demonstrated that there was scant evidence of explicit research on the urban environment. For example, 1.5 percent of urban research conducted in Southern Africa between 1985 and 1992 focused on the environment; 2 percent–6 percent of research in francophone West Africa was on the urban environment between 1983 and 1992; 2 percent of urban research in Brazil during the 1980s dealt with urban environment and quality of life themes, and 4 percent of city-focused research in the southern cone of Latin America had an environmental emphasis during the 1980s (Ford Foundation 1993).

3. An example of this is the Population Crisis Committee's analysis of environmental quality the world's 100 largest metropolitan areas. An "urban living standard score" is developed for each city by combining scores on indicators of public safety, food costs, living space, housing, communications, education, public health, peace and quiet, traffic flow, and clean air. This approach forces the often-arbitrary selection of one value to represent a complex indicator; e.g., public health is assessed on the basis of infant mortality per 1,000 live births, which excluded consideration of the status of adult mortality and morbidity. A second methodological problem is that different data are used for different cities to rank the same indicator; e.g., air quality is measured on the basis of ozone, sulfur dioxide, suspended particulate matter, or nitrogen oxides. Third, to develop a table and rankings without missing variables, the number of indicators was limited to those mentioned above, resulting in the exclusion of important areas such as water quality, open/green space, sanitation, and industrial pollution (Population Crisis Committee 1990).

4. For example, studies have been done on the linkage between environment and health in particular cities. Some representative titles include: Radhika Ramasubban and Nigel Crook, "Mortality Toll of Cities: Emerging Patterns of Disease in Bombay," *Economic and Political Weekly* XX(23), 1985; C. Hertzman, "Poland: Health and Environment in the Context of Socioeconomic Decline," *Health Policy Research Unit Report No. 90:2,*, Vancouver: University of British Columbia, January 1990; Pedro Jacobi, "Habitat and Health in the Municipality of São Paulo," *Environment and Urbanization* 2(2), October 1990; Office of Housing and Urban Programs, *Ranking Environmental Health Risks in Bangkok, Thailand*, Washington, DC: USAID, December 1990.

5. One of the first efforts in this area, the Hong Kong Human Ecology Programme, is a good example of this limitation. It was initiated in 1972; field work was completed in 1975; analysis was completed in 1980; and the results were published in 1981 (S. Boyden, S. Millar, K. Newcombe, and B. O'Neill 1981).

6. For example, the United Nations has collected a set of data for more than 100 cities internationally (UN Population Fund 1988). However, most of it is quite general and does not allow for any detailed environmental analysis. The "Ecoville" project (University of Toronto) generated a number of environmental reports on cities in the developing world during the mid 1980s, but the content and quality of these documents varied greatly, limiting their comparability.

urban development in the Third World because the information and analysis are incomplete, sector based, or outdated. For comparative purposes, past investigations may suffer from these problems *and* not be generalizable to other cases.

1.4   To learn from this recent history and overcome past limitations, urban environmental research that is comprehensive, multisectoral, relatively short term, and consistent between cities is called for. Therefore, one objective of the case study work that preceded this report was to use and test rapid evaluation methods in different cities that cut across sectors. In addition, the work sought to identify generalizable constraints and analytical approaches to problems, outline approaches for setting relative priorities amongst urban environmental problems, and indicate options that could form part of environmental management strategies.

Methodology

1.5   As a methodology, rapid urban environmental assessment draws its inspiration from rapid rural appraisal and participatory rural appraisal. The former, developed during the 1970s, was a "fairly quick and fairly clean" technique for development planning that sought to avoid unsuccessful agricultural projects that were linked to "top-down" and "blueprint" approaches to rural development.[7] The latter, developed during the 1980s, is a participatory approach that involves data collection, analysis, problem identification, ranking of opportunities, preparation of village-level resource management plans, and followup.[8] However, urban assessment is much less anthropological and community focused than its rural counterparts, primarily because cities involve much larger populations and spatial areas.[9]

1.6   A three-step process was developed to enable local (city-based) experts and citizens to assess rapidly the state of the urban environment. This process is based on the need for measurement, observation, validation, and action. To **measure** a consistent set of data, an urban environmental data questionnaire is used. To **observe** the nature, trends, and factors that influence environmental quality in the cities, a common framework for preparing an urban environmental profile has been developed. To partially **validate** and use the results from the questionnaire and profile as a basis for followup action, consultations with key actors in the cities are held. Most important, consultations are a means of reaching consensus and developing political momentum to **act** on priority problems.

Urban environmental data questionnaire

1.7   A common questionnaire has been used to generate a database on a range of environmental information (see Volume 2 for a copy of the questionnaire). The survey instrument was designed over a one-year period (October 1989–September 1990) by a technical working group on urban environmental data, consisting of representatives from a number of international agencies (the

7. See Robert Chambers, "Rapid Rural Appraisal: Rationale and Repertoire." *IDS Discussion Paper No. 155,* Sussex: Institute for Development Studies, 1980.

8. See National Environment Secretariat (Kenya), Egerton University, Clark University, and World Resources Institute, *Participatory Rural Appraisal Handbook,* Washington, DC: World Resources Institute, 1990.

9. An urban community-focused assessment methodology that is more faithful to the rural appraisal approach can be found in Ian Blore, *Guide to the Rapid Analysis of Development in Cities—RADIC* (draft), Birmingham: University of Birmingham, 1993.

UN Fund for Population Activities, Statistical Office, the Department of International Economic and Social Affairs, Environmental Programme, Development Programme, and Centre for Human Settlements; the World Health Organization; the Organization for Economic Cooperation and Development; and the World Bank) and international institutes working in the field of urban environmental research and policy analysis (the International Center for Urban Studies, the International Institute for Environment and Development, the World Resources Institute, the Stockholm Environment Institute, and the Network for Urban Research in the European Community).

1.8   In designing the questionnaire, the working group sought to identify a minimum set of key data that have a high probability of successful measurement in a large number of Third World cities. A number of analytical approaches[10] and relevant survey instruments[11] were reviewed to learn from past experience and avoid redundant data collection. It was concluded that data needed to be collected in the following categories:

- baseline social and economic statistics
- baseline housing conditions
- baseline health conditions
- natural environment
- land use
- urban transport
- urban energy use
- air pollution
- noise pollution
- water resources, water supply, and sewerage/sanitation
- solid and hazardous wastes

Core data were then developed for these categories, with a definition of statistical variables and units of measurement. For example, to describe the predominant ecosystems in and around cities, the Goodall classification of terrestrial and aquatic ecosystems (29 separate descriptors) was selected.

1.9   Data are sought at three spatial levels: the city proper, the metropolitan area, and the urban agglomeration. The city proper is the principal political jurisdiction containing the historical city center. The metropolitan area is a politically defined urban area set up for planning and administrative purposes; it may combine several jurisdictions. The urban agglomeration is the total contiguous builtup area; it may spill over defined political boundaries.

1.10   The categories and indicators were used to develop a draft questionnaire by the UMP, the outline of which appears in Box 1.1. The UMP then provided the resources to field test the

---

10. These included: UN Statistical Office, *Concepts and Methods of Environment and Human Settlements Statistics: A Technical Report*, 1988; European Economic Community, *Green Paper on the Urban Environment* (draft), 1990; World Bank, *Survey of Resource and Environmental Accounting the Industrialized Countries*, 1990; UNEP/UNCHS, *Urban and Regional Environmental Planning and Management Guidelines*, 1987.

11. These included: the questionnaire on "The State of the Environment" used by the OECD/EUROSTAT; the "City Date Framework" used by UNCHS; the ECE's "Experimental Compendium on Envorinmental Statistics in Europe and North America"; the questionnaire for NUREC's International Statistical Yearbook of Large Cities; and the draft UNEP/IEO questionnaire to evaluate national hazardous waste situations.

Box 1.1. Outline of urban environmental data questionnaire

GENERAL INFORMATION

I.   SOCIOECONOMIC BACKGROUND
     (urban population, demographics, income and poverty, employment, municipal services, municipal expenditures)

II. HOUSING CONDITIONS
     (ownership, facilities, size, marginal units)

III. HEALTH CONDITIONS
     (basic statistics, mortality rates)

IV. NATURAL ENVIRONMENT
     (location, ecosystem type, meteorological data, dispersion conditions, topography, environmental hazards)

V.   LAND USE
     (urban land use, newly incorporated urban land, land ownership, land registration, land use regulation, land market)

VI. URBAN TRANSPORT
     (basic statistics, vehicle stocks, motorized travel by mode, emissions, injuries from accidents, passenger car restrictions)

VII. ENERGY USE
     (annual gross energy consumption, emissions from combustion, interconnected electricity grid, in-city electricity utility, urban electricity self-generation, household energy consumption, other indicators, energy pricing)

VIII. AIR POLLUTION
     (emissions intensity, emissions control, policy implementation, ambient concentrations, monitoring, environmental health)

IX. NOISE POLLUTION
     (noise levels, noise pollution control)

X.   WATER AND SANITATION
     (water resources, groundwater abstraction problems, future resources, water supply, water delivery, household sanitation installations, drainage network coverage, sewage flow rates, sewage treatment plants, sewage disposal, industrial effluents, water pollution-policy instruments, water quality monitoring, monitoring)

XI. SOLID AND HAZARDOUS WASTES
     (total solid wastes generated, municipal solid wastes, disposal of municipal solid wastes, municipal expenditures for solid waste management, dump sites, hazardous waste facilities, hazardous waste policies being implemented)

questionnaire in each of the seven case study areas. A local consultant, firm, or group of institutions was identified in each city to complete the questionnaire. They were selected on the basis of a demonstrated experience in environmental and/or urban research, the ability to access information from a variety of public and private sources, and communication skills in English. The names and affiliations of these individuals and organizations are presented in Annex 2. The questionnaire was filled out, transmitted to the UMP/E team at the World Bank, and reviewed to identify problems with consistency, misinterpretation, and missing information. Requests for additional information and validation of questionable data were then communicated to the local researchers and, based on their responses, a final questionnaire was completed. This process occurred between September 1990 and March 1992, depending on the city. On average, two staff months were required to complete, review, and finalize the questionnaire. **The questionnaire is available on diskette with a downloadable database and help screens; French and Spanish translations are also available**. These can be obtained at no charge from the UMP offices in Nairobi and Washington, DC or through one of the regional UMP offices (Accra, Ghana; Kuala Lumpur, Malaysia; Cairo, Egypt; and Quito, Ecuador).

The urban environmental profile

1.11   Although a questionnaire can provide useful baseline data, more description and explanation are required for a fuller understanding of environmental issues in cities. To accommodate this, a draft outline for a generic environmental profile was developed that covers four areas: (a) general background information; (b) the status of the environment in the urban region; (c) development-environment interactions; and (d) the institutional setting for environmental management. This outline was reviewed and modified with suggestions from the UNDP/World Bank Metropolitan Environmental Improvement Programme and UNCHS (Habitat), particularly its Sustainable Cities Programme. A copy of the final generic outline is provided in Box 1.2. Summaries of profiles for all seven case study areas can be found in Volume 2, and full profiles for each city are available from the UMP Programme (approximately 50 pages/profile).

1.12   The **background** section is intended to provide a historical, geophysical, and socioeconomic perspective on urban development for each city and to briefly explain how developmental activities and the environment have interacted over time. The **status** section summarizes existing information on the quality of various environmental media (air, water, land, and cultural property) and briefly analyzes the key natural hazards (both geogenic and human induced) that affect the urban area. The **development-environment** section describes how development-oriented activities and services in the public, private, and informal sectors influence environmental quality *and* how environmental factors constrain or promote development. The **setting** section identifies the key public and private actors engaged in environmental management affecting the city, existing management functions (instruments of intervention used and mechanisms for coordination and decision making), constraints on effective management, and the initiatives that are being undertaken to improve environmental management.

1.13   Preparation of a final profile for each site required a fair degree of supervision and review. To assemble an initial profile, the same researchers who prepared the questionnaire were used in each city. First drafts were based on information from the questionnaire, interviews, existing reports, and other data. These drafts were completely rewritten using a large amount of additional information not cited by the researchers. Second drafts were returned to the researchers for their comments and clarification of inconsistencies. In the case of four cities (Accra, Jakarta, Katowice,

---

Box 1.2. Generic outline for urban environmental profile

I.   INTRODUCTION
     Background
     Geophysical and Land Use
     Socioeconomic Setting (demographics, economic structure, urban poverty)
     History: Environment-Development Linkages Over Time

II. STATUS OF THE ENVIRONMENT IN THE URBAN REGION
     Natural Resources
             Air quality
             Water quality (surface, ground, coastal, fisheries)
             Land   (forests and natural vegetation; agricultural land; parks, recreation, and open space;
                     historical sites and cultural property)
     Environmental Hazards
             Natural risks
             Human-induced risks

III. DEVELOPMENT-ENVIRONMENT INTERACTIONS
     Water Supply
     Sewerage and Sanitation
     Flood Control
     Solid Waste Management
     Industrial Pollution Control/Hazardous Waste Management
     Transportation and Telecommunications
     Energy and Power Generation
     Housing
     Health Care
     Rural-Urban Linkages
     Other

IV. THE SETTING FOR ENVIRONMENTAL MANAGEMENT
     Key Actors
             Government (central, regional, local)
             Private sector
             Popular sector (community groups and NGOs, media)
     Management Functions
             Instruments of intervention (legislative and regulatory; economic and fiscal; direct investment;
             planning and policy development; community organizations, education, training, and research;
             promotion and protest)
             Environmental coordination and decision making (mechanisms for public participation; intersectoral
             coordination; across levels of government; between public and private sectors; intertemporal;
             information and technical expertise)
     Constraints on Effective Management
     Ongoing Initiatives for Institutional Strengthening

REFERENCES

and São Paulo), responses were used to prepare third drafts that were taken to an international conference, World Cities and their Environment, (Toronto, Canada from August 25–28, 1991) where delegates from each of the cities were present. These draft profiles were reviewed with each of the city delegations; corrections as well as new information were obtained. After review by UNCHS, the World Bank and two external reviewers, a final environmental profile for each city was then prepared by the UMP/E World Bank team.

TABLE 1.1. Analytical techniques and applications

Technique	Example of application
Spatial analysis of land use, seismic and other maps	Assessment of open space availability, flood-prone and seismically active areas in Accra
Review of survey data and institutional analyses	Evaluation of functioning of sewerage and sanitation services in Accra
Overlay analysis of maps	Association between waterborne diseases and biochemical oxygen demand in Jakarta
Preparation and analysis of energy balance	Sectoral concentration of polluting fuel usage in Jakarta; air pollution in Tunis
Trend analysis	Growth and shift in peak-hour transport modes in Jakarta
Organizational analysis	Environmental authority by level of government in São Paulo, Tianjin
Long-run marginal cost pricing	Evaluation of degree of cost recovery in São Paulo's water and sewerage charges
Flow chart	Occupational and environmental health data flows in Katowice

1.14 **Specific Analytical Techniques.** Several different analytical tools were used to interpret the information from the case studies, according to the issue that was being assessed as well as the quality and format of the data. The key techniques and examples of their application are presented in Table 1.1.

Environmental consultations

1.15 For the production of paper products (the questionnaire and profile) to go beyond the level of an academic exercise toward action, it must be linked to real-life actors. The process of rapid urban environmental assessment involves three sets of stakeholders: those whose interests are affected by environmental degradation, those who control relevant instruments for environmental management, and those who possess relevant information and expertise needed for addressing a wide spectrum of urban environmental issues. For stakeholders to be involved in the assessment process, they need to be identified, be informed of the process, have a defined role, be provided with a sense of common purpose and collective ownership, and be offered support for their participation. This can be achieved through a **consultation process**, in which a series of discussions are held with the various stakeholders to identify problems, solutions, constraints, and opportunities. These consultations can culminate in an environmental town meeting or forum presided by the mayor or other local executive where representatives of all key stakeholders are brought together in an attempt to reach consensus on priority issues and to build political momentum for followup actions. In light of the 1992 UNCED Earth Summit, this is also a process for developing local versions of Agenda 21.[12]

---

12. Agenda 21 recommends that localities develop their own versions of an environmental agenda for the 21st century. The International Council for Local Environmental Initiatives (ICLEI) is sponsoring a "Local Agenda 21" program that will follow a process that is similar to rapid assessment.

1.16   In four of the cities (Accra, Jakarta, Katowice, and São Paulo), consultations with key individuals and organizations culminating in a town meeting were held to discuss urban environmental problems, priorities, and possible solutions (see Volume 2 for a fuller description of the consultations). In addition to the consensus-building and action-oriented objectives listed above, this process served several purposes: (a) to obtain feedback on the draft profiles and questionnaires from interested citizens in the cities; (b) to acquire additional information from the organizations and individuals that participated in the meetings; and (c) to conduct an *ex post* comparison between priorities that emerged from the analysis of the data and profiles and those that were perceived by the key actors.

1.17   The consultations and town meetings were organized by the "Five Cities Consultation Project" (the fifth city being Toronto) through the University of Toronto's Centre for Urban and Community Studies, an effort that was funded by the Canadian International Development Agency, Department of External Affairs, Mortgage Housing Corporation, and the Urban Management Programme. In each city, a firm or local coordinators was hired to organize semistructured interviews and/or small roundtables with municipal politicians, local government planners, environmentalists, regional/national officials, community groups, universities, nongovernmental organizations (NGOs), and private industry, and to bring these actors together in a final forum to discuss their perspectives and determine whether there was a consensus on metropolitan environmental priorities. The format for the consultations and town meetings was determined by the organizers to accommodate local cultural practices and group dynamics.[13] However, the consultations all covered a minimum common set of issues (water resources, supply and sanitation/sewerage, land use, urban transport, energy use, solid and hazardous wastes, air pollution, and the natural environment), and the town meetings were organized under the auspices of the top local official (mayor or governor).[14]

1.18   A series of consultations were held in each of the cities, concluding in town forums that took place in May and June of 1991 (see following chapter). In Accra, representatives of 33 public and private organizations were interviewed using a questionnaire that covered: (a) the nature of environmental problems; (b) their spatial level of impact; (c) priorities; (d) potential solutions; (e) key actors; and (f) a vision of the city in the year 2010. Following the interviews, a one-day forum was held on May 14, 1991, with 50 government officials, experts, industry representatives, and nongovernmental/community organizations.[15] In Jakarta, the consultation process was based on a series of issue-focused discussions. Three thematic meetings were held on water resource problems and priorities, air pollution issues and options, and housing and the natural environment. These were attended by 27 local and national government officials. They were followed by two larger seminars

---

13. For example, in Jakarta, three roundtables (water resource problems and priorities, air pollution, and housing and the natural environment) and two seminars (hazardous waste and industrial development) were organized to accommodate the large number of actors and to avoid duplication of previous consultation. In São Paulo, institutions and key individuals were contacted separately, both through interviews and questionnaires.

14. Summarized from Patricia McCarney, *Draft Terms of Reference for Local Consultants Working on "World Cities and Environment: A Five-City Consultation Process,"* Toronto: Centre for Urban and Community Studies, University of Toronto, 1991.

15. Summarized from Environmental Management Associates, *Urban Environmental Priorities in Accra: Towards a Strategy for Action,* Toronto: Centre for Urban and Community Studies, University of Toronto, 1991.

FIGURE 1.1. Strategic urban environmental management process

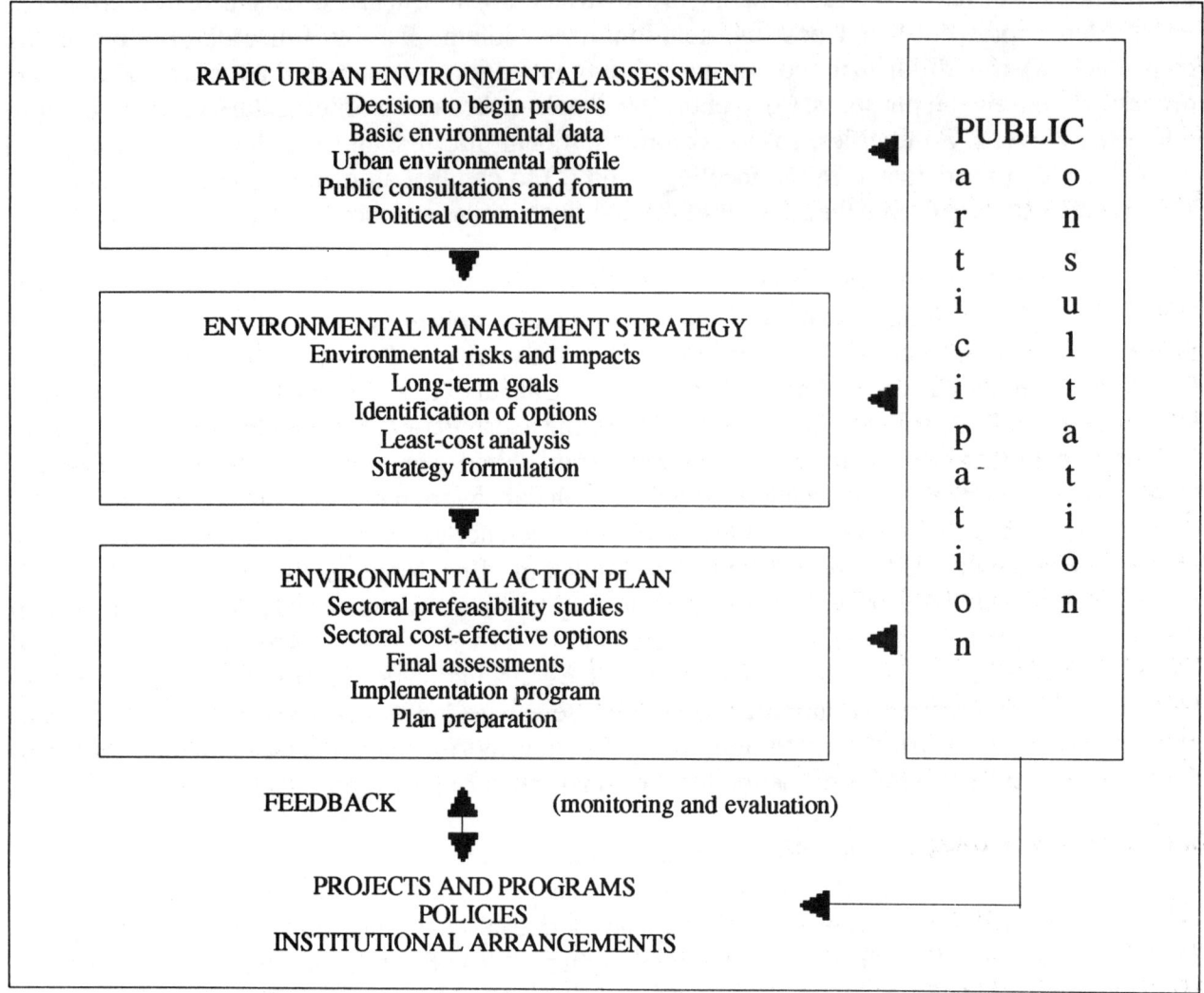

(one on hazardous waste and the other on environment and industrial development) that included private sector and community representatives as well as government participants. The final public forum was a three-day seminar held at the University of Indonesia on June 12–14, 1991; the first two days focused on implementing the clean-river program, and the third day was a general discussion of urban environmental problems and priorities.[16] In Katowice, 29 representatives of regional government offices, industries, and nongovernmental institutions and organizations were consulted. Interviewees were asked to formulate priorities and discuss scenarios for environmental improvement. At the final public forum, held on May 17, 1991, municipal politicians, local planners, local government officials, community groups, NGOs, private businessmen, and academics met to voice their concerns.[17] In São Paulo, initial consultations consisted of interviews, meetings, and small

16. Summarized from Suhadi Hadiwinoto, "The Consultation Process and Environmental Priorities in Jakarta," Toronto: Centre for Urban and Community Studies, University of Toronto, 1991.

17. Summarized from Zdzislaw Schmidt, *Urban Environmental Priorities in Katowice, Poland,* Toronto: Centre for Urban and Community Studies, University of Toronto, 1991.

roundtable discussions involving municipal institutions, the legislative and court system, academic researchers, the private sector, professional associations, NGOs, environmental experts, and community groups. About 50 organizations were consulted, either through discussions or via a questionnaire. This process generated a list of 78 issues that were discussed at a final public forum on May 31, 1991. The meeting, involving 120 people, presented results of the consultations, identified points of consensus, and prioritized problems for followup action.[18]

Rapid Assessment and a Strategic Approach to the Urban Environment

1.19   The rapid assessment process was initially designed for research purposes. However, it can be the first step in a strategic approach to urban environmental planning and management. The technique helps to clarify issues, involve key actors, identify priorities, and build political commitment in a setting where some or all of these elements are lacking. Subsequent steps in the strategic approach are: (a) the formulation of an integrated **urban environmental management strategy** that embodies issue-specific strategies, long-term environmental goals, and phased targets for meeting the goals; (b) agreement on **issues-oriented action plans** for achieving the targets, including identification of least-cost project options, policy reforms, and institutional actions; and (c) a **consolidation** phase in which agreed programs and projects are initiated, policy reforms and institutional arrangements are solidified, the overall process is made routine, and monitoring and evaluation procedures are put in place. These steps are briefly described below and are graphically presented in Figure 1.1; they have been revised and are described in greater detail in a related UMP publication *Toward Environmental Strategies for Cities*. The phases need not be a recipe; for a given city, one might start at the beginning, middle, or end of the process, depending on the existing level of consensus on environmental priorities, as well as political, socioeconomic, and other conditions.

Environmental management strategy

1.20   The process of rapid urban environmental assessment (data collection, profile, and consultations) can provide an informational and consensual basis for preparing an urban environmental management strategy (EMS). The goal of the EMS is to accelerate the improvement of environmental conditions in cities, especially by integrating key aspects of urban policy and environmental management. The objectives are fivefold: (a) establish long-term environmental goals for the urban region; (b) set interim environmental goals and objectives; (c) rank pollution control and other measures to improve environmental quality; (d) identify priority sectors for channeling investments; and (e) recommend policy reforms, instruments, and institutional arrangements needed to implement the EMS. The EMS process builds on existing sector and project work but emphasizes continuity in decision-making to implement agreed policies and approaches. It should provide a decisionmaking framework for public and private investments while recognizing that the investments will be primarily private (by households and firms). It therefore requires a participatory process among decision makers in government and the private sector, often using working groups of officials in consultation with technical specialists and key private and informal sector actors, as they agree and commit themselves to act on the policies and strategies they themselves will define.

---

18. Summarized from Jose Pedro de Oliveira Costa and C.N. Engracia de Oliveira, *Urban Environmental Priorities in São Paulo: Towards a Strategy for Action,* Toronto: Centre for Urban and Community Studies, University of Toronto, 1991.

1.21   The EMS can be developed in a number of different ways but should generally include consideration of health effects and environmental damages (costs), comparison of alternative long-term strategies to achieve environmental quality goals at the lowest economic cost to the urban region, identification of appropriate policies and instruments to implement the least-cost strategy, and an assessment of its institutional and financial feasibility. The final EMS document should summarize the following:

- a review of the environment/development issues, including a complete description of the environmental system from which it originates, the development concerns that are affected, and the stakeholders that should be involved;
- the agreed long-term environmental goals for the urban region;
- a set of interim environmental goals and objectives to guide phased investments;
- the ranking of pollution-control and other measures to improve environmental quality;
- the identification of priority sectors for channeling investments, including project profiles; and
- the recommended policy reform, instruments, and institutional development needed to implement the EMS.

Broad-based acceptance of the resulting strategy requires participation of all stakeholders in this process, including mechanisms for negotiation and conflict resolution. Strategy would require between nine and 12 months.

The urban environmental action plan

1.22   The EMS provides the framework for integration and coordination to ensure consistency across environmental media and sectoral strategies. The third phase of the process is to translate issue-oriented environmental management strategies into action plans, which involves the definition of specific actions for specific actors, complete with time schedules, geographic focus, and priorities. In contrast to the EMS planning process, which is long term and goal setting, action planning is shorter term and implementation oriented. It aims at defining both strategic responses—with specific local government and sector policy reforms together with institutional, legal, and fiscal support programs—as well as an investment program and the elaboration of initial project profiles for short- and medium-term environmental interventions. As with the EMS, action planning is a participatory process that will vary from city to city but should involve the range of relevant stakeholders.

1.23   When the strategic planning phase nears completion, the urbanwide environmental action plan (EAP) can be formulated. The action plan will comprise the set of specific actions that are needed to respond to priority environmental concerns in the city under study. Because these concerns are normally related to specific environmental media and spatial location, the action plan focuses on the coordination and timing of various actions that are needed to address critical problems. In addition to verifying that proposals are consistent with the goals and priorities of the EMS, the EAP also should account for the costs and tradeoffs of competing sector actions. The EAP should not be seen merely as the sum of individual actions taken by the different actors; it should also identify the specific cross-cutting actions required, responsibility for implementing them, and sources of funding.

1.24   The final product of this phase of the planning process will be a set of action plans organized both by priority environmental issues and by responsible actors, as well as a consolidated EAP report. The action plans include recommended projects and supporting actions. The EAP report, in addition to summarizing the agreed strategies and actions, will describe complementary cross-cutting actions and proposed investment programs. It is estimated that preparation, review, and completion of this plan would take between 12 and 24 months.

Sustained investment and institutional development program

1.25   The final phase in this simple characterization of a strategic approach is the initiation of agreed programs and projects, solidification of policy reforms and institutional arrangements, routinization of the overall process, and installation of monitoring and evaluation procedures. Depending on budget constraints and current environmental conditions, a succession of staged investments spread over 15–20 years will be needed to strive for the ultimate environmental quality goals. Success will depend on sustaining both investments and institutional development programs over the long term. The importance of continuity cannot be overemphasized, as gains obtained in the short and medium term can easily be lost by the failure to follow through with needed actions in subsequent stages. Where continuity has been observed, significant environmental improvements have been evident, as in the case of São Paulo. The key activities of this phase are initiating programs and projects to implement the EMS and EAP, building environmental planning and management capacities, and monitoring and evaluating progress. An upcoming UMP publication will provide more details on the EMS/EAP process, along with a review of real-world applications.

Testing and Evaluating the Methodology

1.26   Rapid urban environmental assessment, although inspired by its rural and urban antecedents, does not have any methodological equivalent. Hence, it is difficult to evaluate in comparison to similar techniques because the comparators do not exist. It would not be defensible to directly compare the technique, for example, to its predecessors that were discussed in paragraph 1.4, because it was consciously designed to improve on them. To gauge the utility of the methodology, it was field tested and those results were evaluated against the criteria set out at the beginning of this chapter: is the approach, in fact, comprehensive, multisectoral, relatively short term, and consistent between cities?

Field testing

1.27   The case study approach was selected as the means of testing the methodology partially by default and partly because of the advantages it brings to helping identify appropriate urban environmental interventions. There is no unified theory to explain and predict the dynamics of the urban environment. Consequently, there is no rigorous, theory-driven methodology for conducting analysis in this field. Still, there is a need to collect information, describe observations, and suggest explanations for phenomena in an attempt to establish a pretheoretical, cause-effect framework. Though second-best in comparison with the more replicable and generalizable techniques of theory-based inquiry, the case study method is a valid research tool in the absence of theoretical guidance.

1.28   This argument aside, preparing and comparing cases is a worthwhile approach to problem evaluation for several reasons. First, cases that focus on previously underexplored territory collect knowledge that is based on experience; as lessons from practice are accumulated and assessed, a database becomes available for developing theories. Next, cases allow for observation of a wide range of variables, their interactions, and the outcomes of this interplay. Third, they provide an opportunity to test hypotheses in a number of different settings. Finally, case studies have a nonacademic value: because cases are derived from experience, they are more readily understood by practitioners who are responsible for shaping policy, prioritizing problems, and implementing solutions.[19]

1.29   If the case study method is to be used, then how should one select the individual cases? Criteria for selecting the cities to be used as case studies were derived from several simple assumptions:

- Transnational generalizations will require evidence from diverse geographical, political, and economic settings.

- Urban environmental problems vary according to the level and distribution of a city's wealth.

- These problems also vary depending on the structure and location of a city's economic base.

- Megacities have different and more complex systems for managing environmental problems than smaller ones.

- Rapid data collection and analysis are more readily achieved in cities where work of a related nature is already taking place.

The following selection criteria flow from the above assertions:

- The cities should be selected from different continents, cultures, and political systems.

- They should reflect different levels of per capita income, with varying degrees of poverty.

- They should be characterized by different stages and types of industrialization.

- Both large and smaller cities should be included in the sample.

- Baseline data should be available from ongoing activities in the cities so that primary research can be minimized.

1.30   These selection criteria were combined with a resource limitation to select six cities and one urbanizing area: Accra (Ghana), Jakarta (Indonesia), Katowice (Poland), São Paulo (Brazil), Tianjin (China), Tunis (Tunisia), and the Singrauli region (India). Though Singrauli is not a city, it

---

19. Recently, these and other reasons provided the justification of a case study approach to evaluating environment-development linkaged in rural Africa. See Jonathan Blackwell, Roger Goodwillie, and Richard Webb, *Environment and Development in Africa: Selected Case Studies,* Economic Development Institute Development Policy Case Series No. 6, Washington, DC: The World Bank, 1991.

was selected for two reasons. First, it is a good example of the urban environmental shadow that cities cast on the hinterland (in this case, environmental degradation from urban demand for electricity and coal). Second, it is a rapidly urbanizing region that has a special set of environmental problems. Table 1.2 presents information on these seven areas, organized according to the criteria for their selection.

1.31   The ability to tie into related work was crucial for the process in each city.

- **Accra**—Environmental information has been developed from the UNCHS (Habitat)-supported structure-planning process, known as the Accra Planning and Development Programme, preparation of Ghana's national environmental action plan, the Stockholm Environment Institute (SEI) urban household environment study, and through the World Bank's first urban project in Ghana (completed in 1991) and second urban loan (initiated in 1991).

- **Jakarta**—Related work included activities of the UNDP/World Bank Metropolitan Environmental Improvement Program, the SEI study, and the World Bank's First, Second, and Third Jabotabek Urban Development Projects (initiated respectively in 1988, May 1990 and June 1990).

- **Katowice**—Environmental data have been collected by a number of national and local research institutes in Poland and the World Bank's environmental management project (initiated in 1990).

- **São Paulo**—Urban environmental work has been conducted by the São Paulo state environmental company (CETESB), nongovernmental research organizations and the city government, the SEI study, and a number of World Bank sector loans over a 15-year period (industry, pollution control, water supply, sanitation).

- **Singrauli**—Environmental information has been developed through a number of studies in the region: (a) an environmental impact assessment prepared by Electricité de France; (b) an environmental review by the Indian Town and Country Planning Department; and (c) an ongoing World Bank-supported environmental planning study.

- **Tianjin**—Environmental and background information had been developed as part of the World Bank's Light Industry Project (Report No. 7165-CHA) and the Urban Development and Environment Project (Report No. 10284-CHA), appraised in 1992.

- **Tunis**—The assessment could draw on work of the UN/World Bank Environmental Program for the Mediterranean, the national environmental action plan, and a range of World Bank lending operations for urban development, water supply, sewerage, flood protection, and transportation.

Advantages and limits of the methodology

1.32   Early experiences with rapid urban environmental assessment yielded observations on process as well as substance. This information can be divided into two categories: (a) the utility of

Table 1.2. City characteristics by criteria

Criteria	Accra	Jakarta	Katowice	São Paulo	Singrauli	Tianjin	Tunis
Diversity: Geography	Africa	SE Asia	Europe	S. America	S. Asia	NE Asia	N. Africa
Political & economic systems	1-party/ dereg. to market economy	1 major party/ dereg. to market economy	Democracy/ former socialist economy	Democracy/ market economy	Democracy/ regulated market economy	1-party/ socialist economy in transition	1-party/ market economy
Income:[1] US$ per capita	350	850	4,475	2,540	340+	310	1260
% in relative poverty	48	17	2	37	47	6[2]	18
Industrialization: level and base	Low; agric. products	Medium; manufacturing	High; heavy industry	High; wide-ranging	High; mining and energy	High; wide-ranging	Medium; manufacturing
City size: Metro. population ('000)	1,565	16,828	2,180	16,938	696	8,660	1,558
Related workd	UNCHS Structure Plan; SEI; NEAP; IBRD Urban I & II	MEIP city; IBRD Jabotabek I-III	Local research institutes; IBRD Env. mgmt. loan	CETESB; NGO work; SEI; IBRD loans	EdF EIS: TCP study; IBRD review	IBRD loans	UNDP/ WB EPM; NEAP; IBRD loans

1. The income per capita and relative poverty figures are specific to the metropolitan population.

2. Percentage of population living in substandard housing. No information is available on incomes below the poverty line.

the methodology, and (b) areas that would benefit from further inquiry or different research approaches. For the former set of information, a brief evaluation of the methodology is presented below. For the latter, some thoughts on directions for future research are outlined.

1.33   Briefly, the advantages of the general approach are that it: (a) is rapid; (b) costs relatively little; (c) centralizes diverse information; and (d) benefits from local access to information. On average, the three-step rapid assessment required six person months of efforts over an elapsed period of five–nine months. The local costs for research, writing, and organization of the consultations ranged between $16,000 (Accra) and $27,000 (Jakarta) per city. The research and public discussions led to the centralization of a wide range of environmental information in one place for the first time in each city. Involving local researchers and institutions facilitated access to information and decision makers for a variety of reasons (knowledge of the local language(s) and cultural practices, past experience with the subject matter, relevant organizations and individuals, and established reputation in the field).

1.34   The general methodology also suffered from a number of disadvantages. The first limitation is intrinsically part of the process: the methodology generates purely descriptive information. It provides some guidance as to what might be a priority problem but little to no indication as to what might constitute the range of possible solutions. Second, the approach relies on existing sources of information. With the use of secondary data, results (numbers, analyses and discussions) are confined by the range and quality of work that has already been done. The obverse side of this coin is that the methodology identifies gaps in knowledge. Third, results cannot always be used for comparison between cities because the information applies to different time periods, was derived in a different manner, or is based on a different sample. Finally, the sample of cities in which rapid assessments were conducted is neither large enough nor randomly chosen so as to be statistically representative. Thus, it is entirely valid to argue that many of the conclusions drawn in this chapter are not strictly generalizable to other cities. However, the approach has been used in other cities by other programs so the body of data and application experience is growing; to date, there do not appear to be any significant conflicts with these conclusions.

1.35   Narrowing the critique to each step of the process, the benefits of the **questionnaire** are that it: (a) is a straightforward guide to gathering a comprehensive set of data on a particular city or metropolitan area; (b) brings together data from many different sources and allows for intra- and intersectoral comparisons that are often not possible from a single source of information; and (c) can serve several useful purposes, e.g., by generating information for preparing the profile, the consultations, and intercity comparisons. On the negative side, some of the questions were subject to misinterpretation. A good deal of effort went into correcting these errors and/or explaining the meaning and means of answering particular questions. This may be an unavoidable learning curve phenomenon that does have educational benefits. Also, in each city, certain data were simply not available from secondary sources. This meant that the question or table was left blank, that conversion factors from other cities were used to calculate values (with uncertain degrees of error), or that primary data should have been collected (unfortunately, funds were not available for this option).

1.36   The benefits of preparing the **profile** were that it: (a) summarized information on causal relationships between environmental quality and development activities and the institutional dimension of urban environmental issues that were not collected in the questionnaire; (b) brought together conclusions from reports developed in different sectors or over time that referred to a common problem; (c) and served as a useful background document for, *inter alia*, the consultations, government agencies, NGOs, donors, and others. The principal drawback of the profile is that it was a static document. Each profile had a relatively short lifespan, as no provisions were made to institutionalize the updating of the profile. There were also a set of practical problems, similar to those for the questionnaire, concerning preparation of the document: information was missing; key reports were not available in the city or were not used by the local researcher(s); significant amounts of time and effort were required to explain particular sections and review the draft information; and the quality of the writing itself was often poor. In most cases, the revised version of the profile, which benefited from a literature review process, bore little resemblance to the initial locally prepared research.

1.37   The **consultations** and town meetings had the advantage of being flexible instruments for involving a broad spectrum of concerned publics. Because they were organized locally according to local traditions, they generated meaningful discussion for the participants and allowed them to reach a consensus in each case. However, because the method for arriving at a consensus differed in each case (from subtle negotiation and polite acquiescence in Jakarta to a formal parliamentary-style session in São Paulo), the ability to compare results is limited. More important, the consultation process on which this case study research is based formally ended with the final forum. The consensus was not initially linked to any formal planning or decisionmaking process (though the mayor's or governor's office was centrally involved in each of the town meetings). However, the results of the rapid assessment, culminating in the consultations, were used in different ways in each city: Accra, Jakarta, and Katowice are part of the UNCHS Sustainable Cities Programme, partially because of their involvement in this process; the results of the Jakarta data and consultations were incorporated in the Jabotabek project supported by the World Bank and the UNDP/World Bank Metropolitan Environmental Improvement Program; and the priorities selected by the São Paulo town meeting gave political support to the then-mayor to have the Guarapiranga reservoir included in a World Bank urban watershed project for Brazil. In the future, it would be more effective to associate the consultations more directly with these sorts of opportunities for followup.

Directions for Research

1.38   Some topics that would constitute fruitful areas for future research include (in no particular order of priority):

- **Gathering data on low-income communities**—In many of the cities, most notably Tunis, there was very little information on the environmental conditions of poor people. Data need to be collected at the household and community level to broaden knowledge and awareness about the populations that are usually most affected by urban environmental degradation.[20]

- **Linking health effects with environmental conditions**—In all of the cities except Katowice and Tianjin, there was relatively little information on the cause-effect relationships between environmental problems and their human health consequences. Useful epidemiological and other analytical work could be done on the emissions-dispersion-exposure-health impact pathway.[21]

---

20. Both times series and static data (for intercity comparisons) are needed. The Urban Management Programme has compiled time series data through its urban poverty research in Budapest, Guayaquil, Lusaka, and Manila that can be used to assess environmental condition of the poor. The Stockholm Environment Institute has collected snapshot household and community-level information in three of the case study cities (Accra, Jakarta, and São Paulo).

21. The London School of Hygiene and Tropical Medicine, with support from the ODA and participation of the UMP and World Health Organization, is conducting a study of relative environmental health impacts in Accra and São Paulo. The study is spatially associating mortality and morbidity data with the localized prevalence of particular environmental problems to draw preliminary conclusions in a short time period and target problem areas. The cities were selected partially because of the availability of information generated by this work.

- **Valuing the economic costs and benefits of urban environmental activities**—Reliable values for the productivity, amenity, and other losses and gains associated with environmental conditions and hazards were not available in all of the cities. There are many techniques for calculating the monetary value of these impacts; they could be tested to determine which are most appropriate for different types of problems and levels of available information.[22]

- **Alternative methods of assessing public priorities**—Consensus-oriented discussion is only one of several techniques for developing a sense of what people think is important. Other approaches include revealed preference, contingent valuation and willingness to pay, classic public opinion survey research,[23] comparative risk assessment,[24] and special models for discerning public preferences.[25] These could be tried in the same cities and compared with consultation results or be used in conjunction with consultations in other cities.[26]

- **Relating jurisdictions to ecological boundaries**—More information is needed about the results, limitations, and opportunities for creating or modifying institutions so that their area of responsibility corresponds with the ecosystems that affect them. Research could be done on authorities in cities of developing countries that are organized around water basins, airsheds, waste management areas, agricultural zones, sites of historic or cultural value, and so on.[27]

- **Comparing policy instruments for environmental management**—Cities often adopt similar or different policies to deal with the same type of environmental problem. Why do the same or different approaches succeed or fail? For example, both Jakarta and São Paulo are faced with degradation of their main watershed. Guided land and infrastructure development was a fairly successful

22. The Latin America Environment Division of the World Bank is using contingent valuation and other techniques to assess some of the costs of environmental degradation in certain cities of Latin America. The UMP and the MEIP are planning to test a range of evaluation methods in several Asian cities; as a guide to the literature, the UMP has prepared a paper for this work entitled *Economic Valuation of Urban Environmental Problems.*

23. See, for example, Kathleen Beatty, "Public Opinion Data for Environmental Decision Making: The Case of Colorado Springs," *Environmental Assessment Review* 11, 1991, pp. 29–51; for a developing country city, Layi Egunjobi, "Perception of Urban Environmental Problems: A Pilot Study of the City of Ibadan, Nigeria," *African Urban Quarterly* 4 (1&2), February and May 1989; or, at the developing country level, Riley Dunlop, G. Gallup, and A. Gallup, "International Opinion Toward the Environment," *Impact Assessment* 11, Spring 1993.

24. The US Environmental Protection Agency has been applying comparative risk analysis to urban areas. This approach relies on public participation and technical inputs to set priorities. It consists of: (a) assessment (problem area definition, distribution (equity) analysis, human health analysis, comparative ecological risk assessment, quality of life analysis); (b) planning (ranking issues, setting goals, creating benchmarks); and (c) implementation and monitoring.

25. Several of these exist. A recent application, based on weighting and ranking the discussions and responses of concerned publics, focuses on public priorities as they relate to equity and efficiency in air quality: Climis Davos et al., "Public Priorities for Evaluating Air Quality Management Measures," *Journal of Environmental Management* 33, 1991, pp. 205–267.

26. The UMP and Stockholm Environment Institute have initiated such a study. In addition to a review and summary of the literature, these techniques will be tried and compared through the involvement of the citizenry in several Indonesian cities.

27. The UMP has issued a toll paper that is relevant to this issue: *Urban Applications of Satellite Remote Sensing and GIS Analysis.*

protection policy in Jakarta. Regulation and enforcement of zoning have been near-complete failures in São Paulo.

1.39   Additional topics and refinements will emerge from experience. Since the application in the case study cities of rapid urban environmental assessments (or subcomponents), these have been conducted or initiated in several additional cities, including Abidjan, Bangkok, Bogota, Bombay, Colombo, Côte d'Ivoire (seven secondary cities), Dakar, Karachi, Manila, Mexico (three urban agglomerations); and Rabat.   Some of the organizations that have developed similar approaches include the UNCHS Sustainable Cities Programme, the UNDP/World Bank Metropolitan Environmental Improvement Program, the METAP/MEDCITIES network, the UN Economic and Social Commission for Asia and the Pacific (ESCAP), the German GTZ Urban Environmental Management Guidelines Project (in Nepal and Thailand), and ICLEI's Local Agenda 21 program.

II. PRELIMINARY FINDINGS

This chapter will draw some preliminary conclusions about the relationship between environment and development in the urban Third World. These findings will touch on a number of areas: urban poverty and economic structure, urban institutions and management, and problem analysis and prioritization. Then, some lessons will be suggested for urban environmental management and for research in this area. The managerial implications of this work will be drawn from the preliminary findings.

2.1   Initial results allow for three sets of preliminary conclusions to be drawn based on these case studies. In the area of urban poverty and economic structure, it appears that (a) urban environmental degradation has a disproportionate negative impact on the poor; (b) a city's economic structure shapes many of its environmental problems; and (c) the level of an urban area's wealth is correlated with certain environmental issues. In the area of urban institutions and management, (a) the management of urban environmental problems is complicated; (b) institutions, policies, and environmental problems are not synchronized; and (c) municipal capacity affects environmental quality. In the area of problem analysis and prioritization, it appears that (a) cities have significant extra-urban environmental impacts that require analysis; and (b) public and analytic priorities may differ.

Disproportionate Environmental Impact on the Poor

2.2   Key findings concerning the relationship between urban poverty and the environment can be summed up for each city as follows:

- **Accra**—(a) the poor consume fewer basic resources per capita because of inadequate facilities, services and information;[1] (b) low-income neighborhoods receive the poorest level of service for water supply, drainage, waste collection and sanitation, and pay a higher per unit cost in all cases except for solid waste removal; and (c) the poor are concentrated in high-density areas that are characterized by overcrowded, substandard dwellings.[2]

- **Jakarta**—(a) similar to Accra, the poor are concentrated in high-density, unplanned settlements with semipermanent dwellings, inadequate access to key infrastructure and services, and usually no legal status for the land they are occupying;[3] (b) low-income neighborhoods are exposed to greater risks from

---

1. In high-income residential areas with flush toilets, adequate water supply, and a greater awareness of personal hygiene practices, daily per capita consumption is between 120 and 200 liters. In middle-income areas, the figure is estimated at 100–120 liters per day. However, in slums where water supply is irregular, water is frequently purchased, and levels of health education are low, daily per capita consumption is about 60 liters (Ghana Water and Sewerage Corporation, *Five-year Rehabilitation and Development Plan,* Accra: UNCHS Accra Planning and Development Program, 1988, pp. 62–68).

2. The physically distinct, economically depressed neighborhoods have a population density of more than 350 persons/ ha. and average occupancy rates of 4.4 persons/room. The wealthier areas of the metropolitan region have average densities of 50 persons/ha. and occupancy rates of 1.3 and 1.8 (Jacob Songsore, "Review of Household environmental Problems in Accra metropolitan Area," Paper presented at the Stockholm Environmental Institute, June 1991, pp. 33–34).

3. Budirahardjo and Surjadi, *op cit.,* p. 14.

natural hazards;[4] (c) the poor pay more for lower-quality basic services;[5] and (d) low-cost, targeted investments have improved environmental conditions for the urban poor.[6]

- **Katowice**—(a) relative to the other cities as well as their Polish compatriots, the residents of the voivodeship have less unemployment, a higher income, and less poverty;[7] (b) despite its wealth, the voivodeship has the lowest life expectancy and highest rates of infant mortality, premature births, spontaneous miscarriages, and genetic defects in the country.[8]

- **São Paulo**—(a) low-income residents have the greatest exposure to environment-related causes of mortality and morbidity;[9] (b) at the same time, they have the least access to health care, environmental infrastructure (sanitation, clean water), and environmental services (solid waste collection);[10] and (c) the poor are most likely to be occupants of hazard-prone lands.[11]

---

4. This is particularly true in the northern part of Jakarta, where there are many pockets of poverty. This area experiences (a) regular flooding due to a combination of high tides in Jakarta Bay along with poor drainage during heavy rainfalls, and (b) land subsidence due to overexploitation of groundwater resources and consolidation of the subsoil.

5. In certain slums of north Jakarta, fewer than 15 percent of households had piped water supply; the remainder had access to clean water from peddlers selling 17–27-liter cans from handcarts. This water is priced at an equivalent of US$1.50–5.20/m3; the average tariff for piped water to connected households is $0.10–.50/m3. Thus, depending on market conditions and household distance from the nearest public tap, those purchasing water from vendors may pay up to 50 times more per liter than households connected to the municipal water company. In addition, a recent study indicates that 58 percent of water from handcarts show signs of contamination from fecal coliform (Laszlo Lovei and D. Whittington, *Rent Seeking in Water Supply, Discussion Paper No. 85,* Washington, DC: World Bank Infrastructure and Urban Department, September 1991, p. 7 (1988 figures), and Masulilu, quoted in Budirahardjo and Surjadi, p. 8).

6. Since its inception in 1969, the Kampung Improvement Program (KIP) has focused on upgrading low-income neighborhoods. At a low per capita cost, investments have been made in roads, footpaths, drainage, water supply, public toilets, schools, and health centers. In Jakarta, it is estimated the KIP has benefited 3 million residents over the last 20 years.

7. People in the Katowice Voivodeship have the highest average monthly salary in Poland. The employment rate is more than 50 percent higher than the national average. Because of egalitarian wage and welfare policies of the previous Communist government, there is little relative poverty; in 1990, 2.5 percent of the population was estimated to earn below the poverty line (World Bank, *Poland Health System Reform: Meeting the Challenge,* Washington, DC: Author, January 1992, Statistical Annex, map IBRD 22573; Voivodeship Statistical Office (poverty figures for 1990).

8. Ibid, and Hertzman, *op cit.*

9. For example, environment-related problems lead the list of causes of infant mortality (respiratory conditions and intestinal infections account for nearly half of all infant deaths). Within the São Paulo metropolitan region, infant mortality rates increase as one moves from the richest areas (19/1,000 live births) to the poorest (150/1,000 live births). This relationship is strongly associated with both sanitary conditions and the availability of health care (Joao Yunes and O. Campos, "Health Services in the Metropolitan Region of São Paulo," *Bulletin of PAHO* 23(3) 1989, pp. 351–352).

10. The average availability of hospital beds in the São Paulo metropolitan region was 2.7/1,000 inhabitants in 1985. Disaggregating by neighborhood, the central subregion had 3.1/1,000, and the poorest peripheral areas had only 0.4/1,000. Of the 1,351 outpatient clinics in the region, 73 percent were located in the wealthier central area, and only 0.6 percent were in the northern subregion, one of the poorest (Yunes and Campos, p. 353).

11. In the central subregion, the municipality estimated the 4,800 shacks in 128 slums, representing 25,000 people, run a high risk of destruction from hillside slides (*Shopping News,* São Paulo, August 12, 1990). Flooding is common during the summer, when heavy rains occur. There are 400 areas in the region that are at risk from inundations; an estimated 75,000 people are periodically affected, most of whom are slum dwellers (Celine Sachs, *São Paulo: Politiques Publiques et Habitat Populaire,* Paris: Editions de la Maison des Sciences de L'homme, 1990, pp. 42–43).

- **Singrauli**—(a) 150,000–200,000 inhabitants were resettled in generally substandard conditions following construction of the Rihand reservoir. Residents of these resettlement colonies have poor access to services and suffer loss of social identity; and (b) this condition persists for the 47 percent of dwellers considered to be in poverty, except those in "urbanized villages" owned by public sector firms.[12]

- **Tianjin**—Although income distribution is equitable, wealth-related environmental impacts are not. For example, many city dwellers are residents of slum housing without adequate kitchens, toilets, or waste disposal. Consequently, about one million people are exposed to environmental health risks associated with poorly equipped and maintained public latrines.

- **Tunis**—Low-income communities suffer disproportionately from three types of environmental problems: (a) they are less likely to be connected to sewerage and are exposed to greater sanitation-related health problems; (b) poor neighborhoods have fewer paved roads and fewer regular solid waste collection services, leading to problems with odors and disease vectors associated with uncollected waste or illegal dumps; and (c) they are more likely to be situated in flood-prone areas and are less able to protect themselves from the consequences of flooding.

2.3   From these specific findings, several more general conclusions are posited. First, **the poor suffer disproportionately from urban environmental insults**. Depending on the city and the circumstances, this might result from a number of factors: physical location, inadequate access to health care,[13] environmental infrastructure and services, poor quality of service, and/or overcrowding. Second, **environmentally sensitive and hazardous urban areas are often inhabited by the poor**. These areas are undesirable because of their hazard-prone nature. This means that they either fetch a lower market price and are more affordable to the urban poor, or they have been put off limits in the past and have been illegally occupied by squatters. These situations are often exacerbated by poorly functioning land markets that constrain the supply of safe land, resulting in higher land and housing prices and forcing the poor to marginal areas.[14] Third, **the poor pay more for basic environmental services and infrastructure**. This statement is made on the basis of prices paid per unit consumed. Often, consumption per capita is lower and the quality or reliability of the service or resource is poorer. The costs of compensating for this poorer quality can also be a great burden on

---

12. These conclusions come from a study of nearly 1,500 households in NTPC colonies ("urbanized villages") and rehabilitation colonies (NTPC/EDF/CdF, *Environmental Impact Assessment of Singrauli Area: Land Use*, Chapter 3, 1990).

13. A recent review of more than 100 studies that assessed relations between health and environment in urban areas concluded that "poverty remains the most significant predictor of urban mortality and morbidity" (David Bradley, S. Cairncross, T. Harpham, and C. Stephens, *A Review of Environmental Health Impacts in Developing Country Cities*, UMP Discussion Paper No. 6, Washington, DC: World Bank, October 1991, p. 11).

14. These phenomena are succinctly documented for developing country cities (David Dowall, *The Land Market Assessment: A New Tool for Urban Management*, UMP Discussion Paper No. 4, Washington, DC: World Bank, April 1991; David Dowall and G. Clarke, *A Framework for Reforming Urban Land Policies in Developing Countries*, UMP Discussion Paper No. 7, Washington, DC: World Bank, November 1991).

the disadvantaged.[15] Fourth, **income is not always the best measure of poor quality of life**. This is the main finding for Katowice and Tianjin, where a more equal distribution of income and relatively high level of wealth did not equate with quality of life, as measured by health indicators (not to mention other potential indicators such as the cleanliness and beauty of one's surroundings—characteristics that are sadly absent in both cities). This observation is probably most relevant for cities with current or recently centralized economies that have "egalitarian" distributions of income. Fifth, **targeted interventions can improve the environmental conditions of the poor**. The improvement of solid waste collection and sanitation services to low-income neighborhoods in Accra and the slum upgrading activities of the Kampung Improvement Program in Jakarta are good examples of this point. This is not a new finding but is merely bolstered by evidence from the case study cities.[16]

2.4   What does not emerge from these observations is direct evidence about the full range of causes that the poor suffer the most from environmental degradation. Some of the most evident reasons would appear to be:

- Generally, the poorest members of a community are the most disenfranchised. With little political clout, they cannot articulate their concerns about environmental and other problems, nor can they successfully pressure for solutions.

- The poor have the least economic ability to invest in environmental infrastructure (e.g., septic tanks), hygienic practices (e.g., boiling water), and mitigating measures (e.g., leaving the city during severe periods of air pollution).

- Many of the urban poor have not had access to formal education or are not reached by informal training and awareness campaigns. Thus, they may have a low level of awareness about the causes of environmental problems and alternative solutions.

- Squatter settlements are often on land that is illegally occupied, are difficult to reach, or are unpleasant to visit.

---

15. These points are bolstered by a summation of recent evidence in the *1992 World Development Report* (Chapter 5): "A review of vending in sixteen cities shows that the unit cost of vended water is always much higher—typically from 4 to 100 times, with a median of about twelve—than the cost of a unit of water from a piped city supply. The situation in Lima, Peru, is typical. A poor family pays a vendor $3 per cubic meter, which is more than twenty times what a middle-class family pays for water via a house connection. Thus, although a poor family uses only one-sixth as much water as a middle-class family, the monthly water bill for a poor family is three times that of the middle-class family. In the slums around many cities, water costs the poor a large part of household income—18 percent in Onitsha, Nigeria, 20 percent in Port-au-Prince, for example.... The economic costs of compensating for unreliable services—by building in-house storage facilities, sinking wells, or installing booster pumps (which can draw contaminated groundwater into the water distribution system)—are also substantial. In Tegucigalpa, Honduras, for example, the sum of such investments is large enough to double the number of deep wells providing water to the city. In Bangladesh, for example, boiling drinking water would take 11 percent of the income of a family in the lowest quartile. With the outbreak of cholera in Peru, the Ministry of Health has urged all residents to boil drinking water for ten minutes. The cost of doing this would amount to 29 percent of the average household income in a squatter settlement."

16. For a more comprehensive assessment of the benefits of sites and services, and slum upgrading projects oriented toward the poor, and their impact of environmental quality, see World Bank, *Learning by Doing: World Bank Lending for Urban Development, 1972–82*, Washington, DC: Author, 1983.

- Partly for these reasons, little information is collected to reach decision makers about environmental conditions and consequences in low income communities.

All of these factors make it less likely that poor neighborhoods will receive priority attention from the usually middle-class and upper-class international, national, and local officials who make decisions about investments and policies.

Economic Structure Shapes Environmental Problems

2.5   The structure and location of economic activities in and around cities affect the prevalence and severity of particular environmental problems. This finding appears to be rather trite, but it explains much of the variation in environmental issues between cities. In Accra, with a low level of industrialization and motorization, environmental externalities stemming from these activities (e.g., toxic wastes and ambient air pollution) are less prevalent. To the extent that they are a problem, they are localized as in the case of emissions from the VALCO aluminum smelting plant in Tema. At the other extreme, the priority environmental problems in Katowice are dominated by the side effects of industrial activity and a high level of motorization—air, water, and soil pollution from industrial wastes and vehicular emissions.

2.6   With regard to economic activity, the important variables that influence environmental problems appear to be:

- **Spatial patterns of industrial location and health impacts**—The health effects of industrial pollution are intensified in Katowice and Tianjin, for example, because human exposure to emissions is increased with people living and working in close proximity to sources of pollution. In São Paulo, another relatively highly industrialized city, there is greater separation of industrial and residential areas and less evidence of widespread health problems linked to industrial emissions, though the opposite is true in nearby Cubatao.

- **Ecosystems and industrial pollution control**—Where effective industrial pollution control programs are in place, the contribution of industrial emissions to ecosystem degradation has been reduced (São Paulo and Tianjin). In Jakarta and Tunis, where there are only nascent systems for monitoring and reducing industrial pollution, and in Katowice, where there is sophisticated monitoring but ineffective enforcement, particular ecosystems are being directly threatened (e.g., toxic chemicals in the water and sediment of Jakarta Bay and the forests around the industrial cities of the USIR) or mostly destroyed (e.g., the riverine ecosystems in the USIR) by primarily industrial effluents.

- **Energy use, industrial structure, and environmental impact**—The structure of economic activity, including the transportation system, generates demand for particular types of fuel. The composition of a city's energy balance, as well as the technologies for fuel combustion, result in a profile of energy-related emissions. For example, in Accra, there is little ambient air pollution from the combustion of fossil fuels for industries or transport; instead, there are possibly serious health effects from indoor air pollution due to burning biomass as a cooking fuel, and ecological impacts from intense periurban harvesting of woodfuels.

- **Size and nature of the informal sector**—The economic importance and activities of the unregulated, hidden, or informal economy can have both positive and negative environmental consequences. In Accra and Jakarta, the waste stream is reduced, energy is conserved, and energy-related emissions are reduced through the recycling and resource recovery activities of the informal sector. Conversely, the discharges of hundreds (Accra) or thousands (Jakarta, São Paulo, and Tianjin's township and village enterprises) of small-scale and cottage industries in the informal sector pose a hazardous waste problem that has ranges from the level of the workplace and neighborhood to an entire regionwide effects.[17]

An important aspect of these variables is that they are dynamic. With economic growth or decline, the industrial structure of an urban economy changes, locational patterns shift, the energy balance is altered, and the role of the informal sector changes. This movement over time has important consequences for the range and severity of urban environmental problems.

Level of Urban Wealth Linked to Certain Environmental Problems

2.7   A city's wealth, measured in gross domestic product per capita, indicates that it may tend to have more of certain types of environmental problems. Accra was the poorest city studied, with an annual per capita income of $350, which is typical of many African urban areas. It was the only city where both the analysis and public discussion concluded that **sanitation** was a high-priority issue. In many low-income cities, poor sanitation is an environmental risk because: (a) public authorities have not been able to make adequate investments in human waste collection and disposal; (b) where investments have been made, inappropriate, capital-intensive technologies have often been selected that ultimately cannot be maintained and financed (the deteriorated and underused sewerage system in Accra is a classic example of this phenomenon); and (c) alternative sanitation systems often are not readily available and can be costly.[18] Conversely, some of the problems that plague cities with higher per capita incomes (ambient air pollution and lack of green space) are neither perceived nor assessed to be priority issues in poorer cities.

2.8   The data do not allow for as clear a statement to be made for higher-income cities. From the analysis, it appears that **hazardous wastes** and **ambient air pollution** are priority issues in the range of middle- to higher-income developing country cities. The reasons for this, though, may vary from city to city. Jakarta, considered in the lower-middle-income bracket with per capita income of

---

17. Occupational exposure of workers and family members is a critical related problem in addition to neighborhood effects of hazardous wastes from microenterprises. The numbers affected can be quite large (Bartone *et al.*, 1993; Benavides 1992).

18. For example, moving one step up the income ladder to Jakarta, about 800,000 households have installed septic tanks because of the absence of sewers or other alternatives. These cost several hundred dollars each (not including the value of the land). This is an option that would not be affordable to the average citizen in Accra. This example and the main points are summarized from World Bank, "Sanitation and Clean Water," *World Development Report 1992: Development and the Environment,* New York: Oxford University Press, 1992.

$850/year, is a rapidly industrializing region that is simultaneously rapidly motorizing. However, policies and investments to deal with emissions have not accompanied the growth: policies to encourage treatment of hazardous wastes and reduction of vehicular emissions are only now being studied, and investments in waste treatment facilities, roads, and public transport have not been forthcoming or have not kept up with growth.

2.9   In São Paulo and Katowice, however, industrial output has stagnated or declined in recent years, and the motorization rate has not exceeded the population growth rate. These cities have already reached high levels of industrialization and motorization, and have begun to implement pollution control programs. In Katowice, air pollution is still an important issue because the control programs have been ineffective and distorted pricing policies have encouraged consumption of a polluting fuel. Hazardous wastes have constituted a hidden problem until recently, so solutions have not had time to be developed. São Paulo's geographic setting, which makes it susceptible to climatic inversions, means that even with moderately successful industrial emissions control and vehicular fuel switching programs, ambient air pollution will continue to be a priority problem that will have to be resolved in the future by reducing reliance on private automobiles, enforcing cost-effective vehicle emissions controls, and/or improving traffic management. Hazardous waste has also been a hidden problem, and public pressure has yet to develop to address the issue, as it has in nearby Cubatao.

2.10   In Jakarta, Katowice, and São Paulo, the **lack of green space** (as well as recreational areas) was perceived to be a priority environmental problem, albeit of differing intensity in each city. One explanation of why this is a priority in all cities except the poorest one is that in the wealthier cities, residents have gone beyond a subsistence existence. With surplus time and cash, they can begin to worry about quality of life amenities that go beyond basic needs, such as parks.[19] Another explanation is linked to density: Accra, with 526 people/km² in the metropolitan area, has more open space that is accessible by its population than much denser cities (DKI Jakarta with 12,436 people/km², São Paulo City with 13,100 residents/km², or even Katowice City with four times the density of Accra).

2.11   It is also interesting to consider the problems that are not income sensitive. From the analysis, **surface water pollution** is a high priority environmental issue in all of the cities. The reasons vary from city to city but are not necessarily linked to per capita wealth: in Accra, the problem is driven by poor sanitation; in Jakarta and Katowice, it is a combination of inadequate sanitation and uncontrolled industrial emissions; and in São Paulo, it is primarily a mix of unenforced land use regulations (in the Guarapiranga area) and water-management practices throughout the metropolitan area. From the consultation process, **solid waste** is a top-priority problem in all of the cities except São Paulo. Solid waste collection and/or disposal has not been fully implemented in these cities (though three quarters of the waste is reportedly collected in all three cities); it ascends the priority ranking because it is a visible, daily nuisance. São Paulo, with the highest collection rate (95 percent in the metropolitan area) has less of a publicly perceived problem, although disposal is a serious issue in many cities of the metropolitan area.

---

19. A similar hypothesis was proposed by V.S. Naipaul in *India: A Million Mutinies Now* (London: Heinemann Publishing, Ltd., 1990). His argument is slightly different: having gone beyond a subsistence existence, many Indians had the time and resources to express their cultural differences. Thus, with economic growth, India began to experience an increasing number of ethnic, religious, and caste-related clashes.

The Complexity of Environmental Management

2.12   The management of urban environmental problems is a complicated business. The factors that cause managerial complexity are: (a) the frequently large number of actors per problem area; (b) cross-jurisdictional conflicts; (c) central-local conflicts; and (d) tension between forces for centralization and devolution of authority. The urban environmental management matrix (Table A3-1) provides an initial idea of how particular problem areas such as water, sanitation, and industrial pollution, and certain environmental management instruments such as planning and economic/fiscal instruments can involve a wide range of actors from the central, regional, and local levels of government, the private sector, NGOs, and academia. As noted in the previous chapter, the proliferation of actors involved in a particular sector or problem area, combined with their lack of coordination and communication, have hampered environmental management at the urban level. Examples include: (a) difficulties with: environmental monitoring, policy development, and implementation for Accra; (b) rational resource management and environmental planning in Katowice and São Paulo; and (c) river basin management, solid/hazardous wastes, and participation in local planning in Jakarta. Conversely, when coordinating mechanisms exist, effective environmental interventions can be made at the urban level.[20]

2.13   Many environmental problems cut across political and administrative jurisdictions, making effective management difficult. São Paulo provides an example of this dimension of managerial complexity. For sanitation, there are three cities in the São Paulo metropolitan region where sewage *collection* is a municipal responsibility and sewage *treatment* is the domain of the state government. In these cases, the cities are not treating their sewage and are not connected to the state system. Similarly, municipal solid waste collection and disposal are the cities' responsibility. However, there are cities in the São Paulo metropolitan region with no land available for waste disposal, or that are prohibited from locating landfills because they are in protected water supply catchment areas designated by the federal government. Another example of the managerial limitations brought on by cross-jurisdictional problems comes from Singrauli, where unclear jurisdiction across state boundaries has been the main constraint on effective environmental management and provision of urban services in the region. The states have not been able to work together effectively with national ministries (Energy, Environment and Forests), public sector bodies (National Coalfields Limited and National Thermal Power Corporation), and private corporations to address critical issues of land and water degradation from coal mining, and air pollution from

---

20. The following examples of such coordination embody weak and strong institutional approaches. In Jakarta, several bodies and processes exist to bring together a wide range of different organizations that are working on a similar problem or sector, e.g., TKPP-Tim Koordinasi (the central government interdepartmental coordinating group for urban development), JUPCO (a project management group for the capital city), and IUIDP (a nationwide program for integrated planning). The work of these groups has contributed to the relatively successful implementation of guided infrastructure and land development away from the metropolitan area's ecologically sensitive watershed by shifting growth from the south, where the watershed is located, to an east-west axis. In Tianjin, the Urban and Rural Construction Commission is the municipal government's formal and forceful mechanism for coordinating environmental improvements throughout the metropolitan area. It has successfully managed cooperation between municipal bureaus to: (a) reduce air pollution through the construction of two coal gasification plants to substitute cleaner coal gas for dirtier coal in more than 300,000 households and 1,000 industries; (b) upgrade slums by constructing fully serviced apartment complexes and improve the transportation network by building a series of ring roads after the Tanshan earthquake of 1976; (c) improve water quality by building the largest sewage-treatment plant in China and requiring the installation of 1,225 industrial wastewater-treatment facilities; and (d) significantly reduce industrial solid waste through investments in resource recovery that are partially supported by an industrial pollution-control fund.

electric power plants. Thus, either a "not-in-my-back-yard" attitude or state regulations have prevented these cities from developing alternatives with their neighbors.

2.14   Conflicts between central and local authorities over resources and regulations can also get in the way of effective urban management of environmental problems. Whether a city can tap its economic wealth to invest in environmental control is often determined by fiscal arrangements with the central government. For example, in São Paulo, there was a net outflow of taxes to the state and federal levels prior to the new constitutional arrangements. From 1980 to 1988, only eight percent of federal taxes paid in the city were returned to it and less than one percent of state taxes were refunded. This removal of revenue made it difficult for cities in the Sau Paulo metropolitan region to maintain existing environmental services and infrastructure, let alone finance new investments to meet the needs of a growing population. Inconsistencies and duplication between national and local laws and regulations can also be a barrier to efficient management. As an example, in Jakarta differing legislation has been issued for water quality and effluent standards from different ministries as well as the two provincial governments (West Java and DKI Jakarta). There is also no legislation that specifies which agency(ies) should be responsible for overall river basin management and bringing water quality up to the established standards.

2.15   Whether to concentrate or decentralize the management of a particular environmental problem is part of the complexity. In fact, centralization or deconcentration are not panaceas to environmental management. Attention must be paid, at each stage of a problem, to what level of centralization is appropriate. In Accra, low-income sanitation has benefited from a mixed approach: NGOs and local entrepreneurs have been allowed to operate community improved pit latrines in a **decentralized** fashion. However, desludging and disposal are carried out by the city's **central** Waste Management Department. This has proved to be more effective than operating a completely centralized sewage system that has fallen into disrepair. In Jakarta, **decentralized** community self-help is an important feature of neighborhood solid waste collection.[21] Locally collected solid waste is taken to a transfer station, where it is collected by the city's **central** Cleansing Department. Since 1988, this function has been gradually decentralized through contracting out to private companies. This combination of community collection and centralized transfer/disposal has allowed the city to achieve a relatively high (80%) waste collection rate. Thus, there may not be simple answers to the decentralization debate; more complicated solutions may work.

Institutions, Policies, and Environmental Problems Are Not Synchronized

2.16   Part of the managerial complexity can be attributed to the fact that there is often little relationship between the spatial scale or nature of urban environmental problems and the design of institutions or policies. More often than not, administrative and political jurisdictions do not correspond with ecosystem boundaries or ecological zones. Thus, the processes of planning and implementation can only address partial aspects of environmental problems; for example, there may be an ability to handle waste collection within municipal borders, but solid waste disposal often calls for a metropolitan-wide solution. If there is no metro-level authority to plan, coordinate, and execute a waste disposal program, conflicts and suboptimal results are likely to occur, as in Katowice and São

---

21. In many neighborhoods, people collect monthly dues to support community-organized collection of solid waste. The money is usually used to hire a local garbage collector and to purchase a cart. At least once a month, one member of each household works voluntarily with neighbors to clean the garbage and drainage system in the community.

Paulo. Other areas that can benefit from a harmonization of institutional and ecological boundaries are airshed and water basin management.

2.17   Failure to consider the full ecosystem when designing and implementing solutions to an urban environmental problem can be quite costly and counterproductive. For example, in São Paulo the World Bank financed industrial pollution control projects through the state environmental company (CETESB) and sewage treatment projects through the state water and sanitation company (SABESP). Although both organizations and sets of activities were concerned with improving water quality, neither looked at the integrated problem of water basin management: CETESB was concerned with industrial wastewater and SABESP with sewage. A review of pollution control in the São Paulo metropolitan region noted that this resulted in unnecessary duplication of costly sewage treatment facilities, and underutilization of a public (SABESP) sewage treatment plant in the eastern part of the region because of investment (through CETESB) in private industrial wastewater treatment facilities. An important lesson from the review was the "need for improved coordination…when projects in different sectors potentially impact on one another and on the same geographic area, whether this involves an urban neighborhood or an entire region."[22]

2.18   Similarly, urban environmental problems can be exacerbated when policies do not account for environmental factors. The underpricing of coal as a fuel in Poland has resulted in overconsumption and an absence of incentives to conserve. Environmentally, greater demand for coal has accelerated damages from mining (subsidence and solid waste problems), and inefficient combustion of low-grade coal has worsened air pollution and related health problems in Katowice and other industrial areas. The same can be said for land use policies that fail to prevent building in flood or earthquake-prone areas around Accra, the pre-1985 water-pricing structure in Jakarta that encouraged excess extraction of groundwater, and the unenforceable policy of completely banning settlement and other land development in the Guarapiranga catchment basin of São Paulo.

2.19   Urban environmental management can be an easier and more successful process when physical planning, analysis, and policy development encompass the spatial and other characteristics of vulnerable ecosystems. This was the case in the relatively successful effort to guide land and infrastructure investments in such a way as to encourage growth away from the threatened southern watershed in Jakarta. The Jabotabek Metropolitan Development Plan first proposed ecological zoning for the entire metropolitan area that includes Jakarta. Of the five defined zones, the fifth was classified as a "steep mountainous zone; rapid runoff is limited by vegetation; natural forest areas; agriculture limited to complicated terrace constructions; subject to rapid erosion if forests cleared." This ecological classification then influenced the design of policies and programs to encourage development away from the zone; happily this rational planning was bolstered by physical difficulties in providing infrastructure to south Jakarta and land ownership patterns elsewhere in the metropolitan area. Another example of this synchronization are the municipal provinces in China that encompass major ecosystems. Tianjin is divided into three zones, based on ecological features, geographical characteristics, and economic activities (the Natural Environment and Water Resources Protection zone, the Agricultural Environmental Protection Zone, and the Urban Area and

---

22. World Bank, *Environmental Aspects of Selected Bank-supported Projects in Brazil: The World Bank and Pollution Control in São Paulo*, Washington, DC: Author, Operations Evaluation Department, June 1991, p. 69.

Coastal Environmental Improvement Zone). Different air, water, and noise targets are established and enforced in each zone. Planning is then undertaken at the level of the subzone.

2.20   Several lessons can be drawn from the findings in this and the previous section:

- Efforts to manage urban environmental problems should begin with an ecosystems perspective that encompasses the spatial and cross-sectoral dimensions of the phenomenon. This has implications for the design of institutional arrangements, policies, investments, monitoring, and enforcement.

- Many key institutions, policies, and investments are already in place but were not designed with this perspective in mind. This has partially contributed to the set of issues that complicate environmental management.

- Changing the status quo will be, in most instances, a costly and lengthy exercise. Therefore, in many urban areas, there will be a need for second-best, short-run solutions that do not rely on immediate changes in organizational structure. However, there should be a strong emphasis on medium-term conceptual shifts that embody the synchronization of environmental problems with institutional arrangements and policies.

Municipal Management Capacity Affects Environmental Quality

2.21   Urban environmental quality is also influenced by a city's overall management capacity. If the solutions to certain environmental problems are within the purview of municipal institutions, then these entities must have the necessary financial and human resources. When financial resources are inadequate, as with the case of São Paulo described above, then the maintenance and/or expansion of environmental services and infrastructure will be constrained. On the other hand, when funds are available, municipalities can improve their capacity to address priority environmental issues. For example, German funding for the Waste Management Department in Accra allowed that city to better manage its solid waste problems and initiate a cost-recovery system to sustain services in the future. Sufficient human resources are also critical. Katowice, São Paulo, and Tianjin can monitor their air and water quality in large part because they have the trained staff to do so or can benefit from regionally provided human resources; this is not the case in Accra, Jakarta, and Singrauli. So even if cities' authorities can develop environmentally aware institutions, policies, and programs, they must have the capacity to fund and manage these initiatives.

2.22   When cities do not have the capacity to manage particular problems or fail to exercise existing capacity, then citizens can and have relied on nonmunicipal solutions to address urban environmental issues. For example, in many developing country cities, individuals and enterprises in the informal sector earn a living through resource recovery of recyclables in the solid waste stream, both at the collection and disposal stages; this is the case in Accra, Jakarta, and the Singrauli region. Community groups often get involved in service delivery when city services do not reach a neighborhood: in Accra, low-income communities have organized to provide their own sanitation facilities because the city's limited sewer system does not reach them; in Jakarta, many neighborhoods have organized their own solid waste collection and removal to areas where the municipal service does collect. In these informal sector and community examples, the city administration may condone but does not officially support the activities. However, municipalities can consciously work with these unofficial service providers on a formal, contractual basis to expand coverage. This happens more frequently through the formal private sector, as with the case of private provision of solid waste collection and disposal in São Paulo.

Public versus Analytic Priority Setting

2.23   Two important outcomes of the final town meeting in each of the cities were (a) the emergence of a set of criteria for prioritizing urban environmental problems and (b) the identification and prioritization of those problems. The following criteria for prioritizing problems have emerged from the application of the rapid assessment technique:

- the magnitude of health impacts associated with the problem
- the size of urban productivity losses caused by the problem
- the relative impact of the problem suffered by the urban poor
- the degree to which the problem results in or is caused by unsustainable consumption of resources
- whether or not the problem leads to an irreversible outcome
- the extent to which local support or a constituency exists to support resolution of the problem.

The information required to apply the first five criteria may need to be further developed during preparation of an environmental-management strategy (see previous chapter). The results of the consultations can be a useful guide for applying the final criterion. These criteria can also be used to evaluate policy, programmatic, institutional, and investment options, and to evaluate outcomes.

2.24   Each forum reached consensus on a priority list of issues. The length and detail of each list varied from city to city, but it was possible to standardize the listings to arrive at a set of eight high-, medium-, and low-priority problems. These rankings are presented in Table 2.1. Some of the meetings went beyond the prioritization exercise and discussed limitations and strategies for environmental management. In considering the results in the table, an important caveat is in order: the rankings do not necessarily reflect public opinion. They stem from a process based on participation by interested, involved, and affected segments of society. Thus, the consultations were a means of eliciting opinions, facts, and ideas from these specialized "publics." However, a statistically valid snapshot or time series public opinion survey might yield a different hierarchy of priorities. Therefore, "public" is used in a very limited way in this discussion.

Analysis-based priorities

2.25   It may be possible to derive a more analytic ranking of the environmental problems in these cities using data and information in the questionnaires and profiles. In an attempt to do so, a matrix was prepared to assess the types of problems that were identified in Annex 3 (see Table A3.2): air-related problems (ambient and indoor pollution), water-related problems (surface, groundwater and coastal/lake), cross-media problems (solid waste, hazardous waste, environmental hazards, poor sanitation), and other problems (e.g., occupational safety, noise pollution). The severity of these problems can then be ranked according to the criteria outlined at the beginning of this section—health impact, economic losses, impact on the urban poor, irreversibility, unsustainability of resource

Table 2.1. Environmental priorities from the consultation process

Problem Priority	CITY			
	Accra	Jakarta	Katowice	São Paulo
High	Inneffective land use controls	Poor solid waste management	Inadequate public awareness	Substandard housing
	Poor solid waste management	Groundwater pollution	Industrial pollution and structure	Lack of urban infrastructure for poor
	Inadequate sanitation	Surface/bay water pollution	Solid & hazardous waste pollution	Settlement of risk-prone areas
	Poor drainage	Air pollution	Air pollution	Limited green space
Medium	Insufficient housing and green space	Substandard housing	Water pollution & inadequate supply	Inadequate sewage treatement
	Poor transport management	Poor transport management	Inadequate sanitation	Water supply not protected
	Low awareness	Deteriorating public utilities	Lack of green space/ clean soil	Flooding
Low	Industrial pollution	Inadequate social infrastructure	Poor transport management	Vehicular air pollution
	Environment not part of planning	Lack of green and open spaces	Energy-related pollution	Poor transport management

consumption, and degree of local support. A simple scale (1 = low impact; 2 = medium impact; 3 = high impact) was applied for each problem and set of criteria; the rankings were then totaled to derive a score for each problem (lowest possible score = 0; highest = 18). Once rankings were prepared for each city, they were divided into high-, medium-, and low-priority areas. A problem area that scored 13 or more points was labelled high priority, with a rating of 7–12 points constituting a medium-intensity issue, and low-priority being less than seven points. This resulted in a potentially more analytic set of rankings that are summarized in Table 2.2.

2.26   This type of analysis is an initial attempt at a more transparent, empirical and analytical assessment of urban environmental problems, as compared to the more impressionistic and subjective ranking that emerged from the consultation process. However, several factors limit the actual objectivity of what appears to be a rational ranking process: (a) data on impacts were inconsistent between cities (e.g., mortality figures were available for Katowice and São Paulo, but only morbidity data could be obtained for Accra and Jakarta); (b) data were often unavailable, especially concerning the economic costs of particular problems—in such instances, an educated guess was substituted for hard information; (c) some criteria may deserve greater weighting than others, whereas this approach is equiscalar; and (d) the list of problems assessed (even with the option of an "other" category) do not represent the universe of potential urban environmental issues. The

Table 2.2. Data and criteria-based problem ranking

Ranking/City	Accra	Jakarta	Katowice	São Paulo
High (13+ points)	Poor sanitation	Ambient pollution	Surface water	Surface water
	Surface water	Surface water	Ambient pollution	Environmental hazards
		Groundwater	Hazardous waste	Forest/agriculture
		Poor sanitation	Solid waste	Hazardous waste
				Poor santitation
Medium (7–12 points)	Environmental hazards	Hazardous waste	Groundwater	Ambient pollution
	Indoor pollution	Ambient pollution	Forest/agriculture	Solid waste
	Rural ecosystems	Coastal pollution	Environmental hazards	Noise pollution
	Hazardous waste	Environmental hazards	Job safety/health	Coastal pollution
	Coastal pollution	Forest/agriculture	Indoor pollution	Indoor pollution
	Forest/agriculture	Cultural property	Cultural property	
	Solid waste	Rural ecosystems	Poor sanitation	
	Groundwater	Solid waste	Rural ecosystems	
Low (<7 points)	Cultural property	Indoor pollution		Rural ecosystems
	Ambient pollution			Cultural property

set of problems that were evaluated emerged from the analysis and were limited to making the analytical exercise more manageable.

Comparing public and analytical priorities

2.27 Despite the limitations of the approach, it is interesting to compare the listings to see if and where they differ or coincide. In Accra, the analysis indicated that surface water pollution was a high priority problem; however, only one aspect of this issue was on the public high-priority list (drainage). Conversely, a publicly identified top priority (ineffective land use controls) was not even part of the range of analyzed problems. In Jakarta, poor sanitation was high on the list of analyzed problems; the town meeting addressed it as only part of a medium-priority issue (deteriorating public utilities). In Katowice, surface water pollution was high on the analyzed list but was only a medium-level problem from the consultation process; however, an issue that was not even included in the analysis topped the public priority list (inadequate public awareness). In São Paulo, only one issue was in common on the two top-priority lists (environmental hazards/settlement of risk-prone areas). Again, high-priority issues were identified in the town meeting that were not included in the analysis (substandard housing and the lack of urban infrastructure for the poor). In all of the cases, the public forums identified poor transport management as an important environmental problem; however, it was not considered in the "objective" analysis.[23]

2.28   Some of the conclusions that can be drawn from this comparative exercise are:

- **No optimal ranking method**—The public system of identifying and setting priorities is limited by time, access to information, a lack of stated objective criteria, and only a subjective means of comparing different types of problems. The analytic approach suffers from an absence of consistent data, failure to incorporate all of the publicly perceived issues, and a potentially arbitrary ranking system.

- **Bias of public process**—The high-priority problems identified by the consultation process tended to be those that were visible (e.g., solid waste, air pollution, substandard housing) or that had been well publicized (e.g., poor drainage, groundwater pollution, settlement of hazardous areas). This leads to an under recognition of risks that are not physically apparent or fully documented, such as hazardous wastes.

- **Bias of analytic process**—The analysis tended to focus on some of the more quantifiable concerns, partly because measurements and reports were available on, *inter alia*, air and water quality.

- **Potential for complementarity**—Public discussions can broaden the focus of analysts and decision makers by raising issues that might not arise in a standard analysis, for example, the attention to process (land use controls in Accra or inadequate public awareness in Katowice) or a particular sector that is plagued with environmental problems (substandard housing in Jakarta and São Paulo). An advantage of the analytic approach is that it may center public attention on problems that are real but the existence or impact of which is not perceived by the public (e.g., hazardous waste in the case of São Paulo).

Cities Have Significant Extra-urban Environmental Impacts

2.29   Urban demand for natural resources and the disposal of city wastes that result from resource transformation can harm environmental systems outside of the city proper. The Ghana hydropower case in the previous chapter is one example of this phenomenon. Others include: (a)

---

23. The potential for divergence between expert and public opinion concerning environmental priorities is reinforced elsewhere. For example, in the United States, specialists from the American Society of Mechanical Engineers ranked solid waste management and hazardous/toxic wastes as the two top environmental problems, with air and water pollution tying for third. The public ranked air pollution at the top of the list, hazardous waste second, and water pollution third; only 20 percent of the public thought solid waste was a priority problem (Robert Lichter and D. Amundsen, *Solid Waste Management: Comparing Expert Opinion, Media Coverage, and Public Opinion*, Washington, DC: Center for Media and Public Affairs, 1992).

accelerated deforestation around Accra that is stimulated by urban household demand for wood and charcoal; (b) water resource and land use conflicts that are affecting agricultural production in West Java; (c) pollution of waterways throughout the voivodeship from industrial and municipal wastes generated principally in the upper Silesian industrial region; and (d) an increase in coastal pollution from wastes originating in São Paulo. If the level of analysis is limited to the city proper, then these environmental problems that occur outside of metropolitan boundaries will not be taken into account.

2.30   In a similar vein, not all extra-urban environmental effects are entirely negative. The Ghana hydropower case is an example of a situation with both positive and negative environmental, economic, and health impacts. The capacity of cities to absorb (to varying degrees of success) burgeoning rural populations can have positive environmental consequences outside of the urban area. In Brazil, the argument is that if villagers and town dwellers did not have the opportunity to migrate to cities such as São Paulo, they would either remain where they are and put increasing pressure on rural water, soil, and other resources, or they would migrate to frontier areas and contribute to the destruction of Amazonian rainforests or other fragile ecosystems. So it is also important to recognize the possible positive environmental effects that urban areas can have on the hinterland. This dynamic will continue as long as São Paulo, for example, can continue to provide better opportunities and a higher quality of life than are perceived to exist in the countryside, thus reinforcing the need for effective urban environmental management.

General Findings for Urban Environmental Management

2.31   These findings offer a potentially rich source of advice for those seeking to improve environmental management in Third World cities. The following general findings flow from the preliminary lessons cited above:

- **Urban environmental strategies should have an explicit focus on the problems of the poor.** As the urban poor suffer disproportionately from environmental insults, their environmental problems should be more heavily addressed in the development of policies and programs. The findings suggest that the poor are willing to pay for environmental services and infrastructure, they are already often paying more than the well off, and targeted interventions can improve environmental quality in low-income communities.

- **City-specific strategies should be guided by the configuration of key economic variables.** These variables are: (a) the level of industrialization (focusing on the exposure of different populations to high-risk emissions and the extent to which effective pollution-control policies are in place); (b) the composition of the energy balance and its dynamics, as an indication of energy-related emissions; and (c) the positive and negative environmental roles of the informal sector.

- **Solutions that are not heavily dependent on institutional performance may be necessary in the short run.** Because of the factors that complicate environmental management, building institutional capacity will take time. While sound economic policies that internalize the costs of environmental externalities should be pursued, second-best alternatives may be required in the near term. For example, crude but easy-to-collect gasoline surcharges may be a more effective instrument to reduce downtown congestion and pollution than the enforcement-intensive Singaporean permit system for peak periods.

- **Enhanced public awareness, consultation, and participation can improve environmental management.** The divergence between public and analytic priorities indicates that environmental education may be needed to raise public consciousness about hidden problems. The consultation process showed its value in identifying a number of topics, including process-oriented issues, that had not been developed through the top-down analysis. Participation in implementing environmental solutions, particularly for problems that manifest themselves at the neighborhood and community level, was important in several of the cities.

- **Pay careful attention to the relationship between problem areas, their spatial scale, and institutional capacity when designing interventions.** The impact and importance of different problems will vary between cities and over time. Empirical evidence may lead to different conclusions than public opinion. The spatial dimension of problems may not correspond to jurisdictional or sectoral alignments, and impacts can extend well beyond metropolitan boundaries. The availability of financial and human resources will condition local capacity to manage environmental problems.

These summary observations all point to a final conclusion: each city represents a singular combination of conditions, problems, constraints, and opportunities for environmental management. Thus, although common criteria may be used to evaluate problems and set priorities in a range of cities, a unique strategy will have shacks in 128 slums, representing 25,

ANNEX 1. VOLUME 2: TOOLS FOR RAPID URBAN ENVIRONMENTAL ASSESSMENT

Contents

ANNEX 2. LIST OF LOCAL CONSULTANTS AND INSTITUTIONS

ACCRA

Dr. A.T. Amuzu — Assistant Director, Water Resources Research Institute, and Director, Environmental Management Associates

JAKARTA

Suhadi Hadiwinoto — National Project Coordinator, UNDP/World Bank Metropolitan Environmental Improvement Program, and Former Chief, Environment and Infrastructure Division, Jakarta Regional Development Planning Board
(Mr. Hadiwinoto was assisted by Dr. Giles Clarke, consultant to the UMP)

KATOWICE

Dr. Jerzy Borkiewicz — Director, Institute of Material Economy

Dr. Ewa Mieczkowska — Chief, Department for Utilization of Industrial Waste, Institute of Material Economy

Dr. Alicja Aleksandrowicz — Research Scientist, Institute of Material Economy

SÃO PAULO

Celso N.E. de Oliveira — Professor, School of Public Health, University of São Paulo

Arlindo Philippi — Head, Pollution Control Program Department, CETESB (State Environmental Protection Company)

SINGRAULI

Dr. Ranjan Bose — Tata Energy Research Institute, New Delhi

TIANJIN

Ms. Guo Lian-cheng — Director, Environmental Protection Information Center, Tianjin Environmental Protection Bureau

Qin Bao-ping — Division Head, Tianjin Environmental Monitoring Center

TUNIS

Abdelkader Baouendi — Director, National Environmental Protection Agency (NEPA)

Hedi Larbi — Cofounder, Engineering Company for Economic and Social Development (SIDES)

Ahmed Basti — Senior Engineer, SIDES

Mohamed Hentati — Director, Prevention and Control Department, NEPA

ANNEX 3. SYNTHESIS OF SUBSTANTIVE RESULTS

A3.1   This annex reviews the substantive results from the case study areas that were generated by the rapid assessments, particularly the questionnaires and profiles. Comparisons are made and tentative conclusions are drawn concerning: (a) the status of the environment in the urban region; (b) the interaction between urban development and the environment; and (c) the institutional setting for environmental management. This structure follows the organization of the environmental profiles (see Box 1.2).

Status of the Environment in the Urban Region

A3.2   Two areas are evaluated to describe the status of the urban environment: the quality of environmental systems and the presence of environmental hazards. Environmental systems revolve around the triad of environmental media—air, water, and land. Environmental hazards at the city level, also referred to as urban vulnerability, are risks that are exacerbated by natural events or human activities. Conclusions concerning these two areas are presented below.

Quality of environmental systems

A3.3   In this section, findings are presented about the factors that influence the quality of environmental media in the case study cities. To simplify the presentation, three environmental systems are categorized: air, water, and land. *Air* refers to the principal airshed that covers the central city; it includes both ambient and indoor air quality. *Water* incorporates surface, ground, and coastal resources, including fisheries. *Land* groups agricultural and forested areas, open/recreational space, cultural/historical property, and land used for the disposal of solid and hazardous wastes.

A3.4   **Air.** The key findings concerning the quality of urban airsheds are:

- **As income and the level of industrialization increase, air quality worsens and the mix of air pollutants changes.** Much of this can be attributed to the intensity and composition of energy use (described below in the section on development-environment interactions). For example, in the lowest income/ least industrialized city (Accra), vehicular and industrial air pollution from combustion of commercial fuels is insignificant, but indoor air pollution from burning biomass fuels for cooking and water heating is a potentially serious health problem. In the highest income/most industrialized city (Katowice), air pollution from vehicles and industries using commercial fuels is serious, while there is no problem related to biomass combustion.[1]

- **Topography, climate, and meteorology are important variables that affect air quality.** For example, coastal breezes play a key role in flushing air

---

1. Analysis of a larger sample indicates that urban concentrations of certain pollutants (particulates and sulfur dioxide) initially increase with income and then begin to rapidly decrease (World Bank, *World Development Report 1992: Development and the Environment,* Washington, DC: Author, 1992, p. 11). The sample in this study was not large enough to capture this effect.

pollutants from Accra, Jakarta, and Tunis. São Paulo's inland, hilly location and colder winter season lead to serious air pollution during the frequent winter inversions. Prevailing wind patterns subject the city of Katowice to air pollution from elsewhere; 60 percent–70 percent of air pollution in the city originates from elsewhere (mostly in the Upper Silesian industrial region).

- **Motorized vehicles or low-quality fuels are the most significant source of many air pollutants.** In Katowice, 75 percent of lead emissions are from vehicles. In Jakarta, motorized transport is the key source of air pollution, with much of effluents (including all of the suspended particulate matter from mobile sources) originating from trucks, buses, and motorized two- or three wheelers. In São Paulo, vehicle usage produces 94 percent of carbon monoxide, 89 percent of NO_2, 77 percent of hydrocarbons, and 73 percent of SO_2. In Singrauli and Tianjin, the combustion of coal by industries, power plants, and households accounts for much of the air pollutants.

- **Particular segments of the urban population face higher health risks from exposure to air pollutants.** In Accra, people who spend more time at home (women, children, and the elderly) are more exposed to indoor air pollutants from the combustion of cooking fuels. In Jakarta, commuters, bus drivers, and schoolchildren are exposed to higher concentrations of lead and carbon monoxide. In Katowice, certain schoolchildren, hospital patients, apartment dwellers, and babies at nurseries are part of the high-risk exposure group because of their proximity to factories, power plants, coal heaps, roadways, and other sources of air pollutants. In Tianjin, atmospheric pollution and unhealthy workplace conditions result in higher occurrences of environment-related diseases for residents in the northwest and eastern parts of the city.

A3.5	**Water. Surface waters**, important sources of drinking and industrial water, are being increasingly contaminated by industrial, solid, and human wastes. This conclusion holds for all the cities, although the nature and location of the problem varies by city: Accra's lagoons are primarily polluted by untreated human excreta and secondarily by industrial effluents; in Jakarta's important Sunter River system, 50 percent of biochemical oxygen demand (BOD) originates from industrial and other wastewater, 15 percent from solid waste, and 19 percent from domestic sewage; in the Katowice voivodeship (governorate), where less than 2 percent of the length of all waterways are deemed suitable for providing fresh or raw drinking water, communal sewage accounts for 43 percent of water pollutants, with industrial sources (particularly wastewater from mining) making up the majority; the three most important rivers serving the São Paulo metropolitan region are affected by urban sewage and industrial wastewater that result in high levels of fecal coliform, BOD, nitrogen, and phosphorus, and the two key reservoirs have excess dissolved oxygen, toxic substances, and fecal coliform counts; Singrauli's key source of water, the Rihand Reservoir, is threatened by runoff from fly ash ponds and mining operations; in Tianjin, most streams, channels, and canals are polluted by high levels of COD (chemical oxygen demand), algal blooms, heavy metals, and salt; Tunis is confronted with industrial pollution in the southern part of the Lac de Tunis as well as sanitation problems from settlements in the watershed that can affect drinking water quality.

A3.6   **Groundwater** resources are increasingly threatened by overexploitation or inadequate protection in Jakarta, Katowice, Singrauli, and Tianjin; the aquifer is not a major source of water in the other cities. In Jakarta, Katowice, and Tianjin, overexploitation has resulted in the salinization of the groundwater supply and has contributed to land subsidence; Tianjin has responded with a program to recharge the aquifer. In Jakarta, the resource has been further contaminated by seepage from poorly maintained septic tanks. In Katowice, leaching from the area's many waste dumps has added to groundwater pollution. In Singrauli, all groundwater tests have failed to meet drinking water standards due to fecal contamination and the presence of heavy metals.

A3.7   **Coastal water** pollution is a problem in all of the coastal cities (Accra, Jakarta, Tianjin, and Tunis). High levels of total and fecal coliform have been measured along the Accra beachfront of the metropolitan area, and linked to disposal of untreated sewage. A similar situation exists in Jakarta and is compounded by the presence of heavy metals in the sea sediment and waters of Jakarta Bay from industrial and vehicular emissions. In both cities, it has been hypothesized that this coastal pollution has had an adverse effect on fisheries; however, no measurements have conclusively proved this link. Tianjin's coastal waters suffer from excess COD, eutrophication, and petroleum pollution; a decline in marine fishing has been documented and attributed to this pollution as well as overfishing. In Tunis, the discharge of partially treated sewage into Mediterranean waters has adversely affected fisheries, recreational opportunities, and tourism.

A3.8   **Land.** In the case study cities, **agricultural activities** are affected by two types of urban activities. In Accra, Katowice, and Tianjin, produce is often polluted by pathogens from the use of sewage irrigation in Accra and Tianjin (where 25 percent of agricultural lands are irrigated with sewage) or heavy metals from industrial and power production in Katowice. The soil around Tianjin is also polluted and depleted from heavy use of chemical fertilizers and pesticides. In Jakarta, São Paulo, Singrauli, and Tunis, agricultural production is declining or insignificant, as fertile lands have been converted to higher value end uses, e.g., residences, roads, mines, and industrial or commercial areas. Periurban **forested land** has been reduced in most of the cities, but for very different reasons: currently in Accra and previously in Jakarta, deforestation has been linked to demand for biomass energy; in Katowice, tree loss has been accelerated by industrial air pollutants; in São Paulo, the primary cause of reduced forest resources has been land clearing by developers of illegal settlements; in Singrauli, 16,000 ha. of forests has been destroyed since 1981, primarily because of open-cast mining and related soil erosion. Only in Tianjin has this situation been reversed: 15 percent of urban land is classified as green space, partly because of active tree planting and forest conservation programs. In all cities, illegal or poorly managed **solid and hazardous waste disposal** has contributed to land degradation.

A3.9   The key findings concerning open and recreational space are that: (a) the denser, more industrialized cities have relatively little green space per capita (1 m² in Tunis, 2.3 m² in Tianjin, 4.5 m² in the São Paulo metropolitan region, compared to the World Health Organization recommendation of 11 m²; and 18.2 m² in Katowice compared to the Polish national average of 24.8 m²); and (b) different factors are given for the inadequacy of urban recreational space (a lack of planning and protective zoning in Accra and Katowice, demographic pressure in Jakarta, failure to enforce open space plans in Tunis (illegal settlements occupy 20 percent of areas designated as green space), and pollution of potential recreational areas, such as the reservoirs, in São Paulo). **Cultural and**

historical properties have been effectively preserved in Accra (colonial forts and castles), Jakarta (the old port and administrative areas), and Tunis (the Medina) through continued occupation and use or by their development for tourism (the Carthage architectural park in Tunis). In Katowice, there is evidence that historic buildings and monuments are being damaged by corrosive air pollutants, and those located near mining activities are subject to structural damage from land subsidence. In Singrauli, three major architectural and historical sites have been catalogued, but no preservation plan is in effect.

A3.10   Finally, environment-related **land conflicts** occur in several of the cities: in Accra, spilling of reservoir water inundates salt works in the coastal wetlands while the saltponds accelerate coastal erosion and increase soil salinity, making the soil unsuitable for agriculture; in Jakarta, rice production north of Tanggerang is increasingly restricted because of water shortages as upstream abstraction of water increases for urban use, and residential development has moved farmers to ecologically sensitive areas of the southern watershed, leading to more soil erosion and related problems; in Katowice, many land uses are affected by coal, zinc, lead, and sand mining that is expected to visibly damage 12 percent of the voivodeship's area by the year 2010; Singrauli has experienced significant land use conflicts from construction of the Rihand Reservoir, which displaced 150,000–200,000 people, mining activities, and the influx of migrant workers.

Environmental hazards

A3.11   All the cities, except Katowice and Singrauli, are variably affected by natural hazards. Key environmental sources of risk for their urban citizens are the following:

- **Flooding** is a seasonal problem that affects particularly low-income neighborhoods in Accra, Jakarta, and São Paulo; it is aggravated by the impermeabilization process that occurs with urbanization. The most serious floods usually extend beyond slums, resulting in deaths and high economic costs, as in Accra on May 4, 1986, São Paulo on March 19, 1991, and a number of events in Tianjin (1953, 1955, 1964, 1977, and 1978).

- **Soil structure** makes many neighborhoods in Accra prone to waterlogging, with associated environmental health problems. Soil composition is also linked to occasional landslides in São Paulo, with resulting loss of life and property.

- **Earthquakes** have seriously affected the residents of Tianjin and, to a lesser extent, Accra. In 1976, the Tanshan earthquake caused 30,000 deaths and destroyed or damaged much of Tianjin's old building stock and infrastructure. For Accra, earthquakes are an infrequent occurrence with medium- to large-scale events every 30-60 years.

- **Coastal erosion** in Accra is due to continuous strong wave action affecting the city's narrow continental shelf, resulting in increasingly serious property losses. In Tunis, this erosion has damaged infrastructure and beaches.

In Katowice, land subsidence is sometimes referred to as a natural hazard but, in fact, it is due entirely to mining activities and overexploitation of groundwater resources.

A3.12   Many of the so-called "natural" hazards are often exacerbated by human activities. For example, land subsidence caused by overexploitation of groundwater is a problem in Jakarta and Tianjin, as well as in Katowice. Extensive damage from earthquakes in Accra has been attributed to the construction of buildings that cannot withstand the tremors. Similarly, unenforced building codes have worsened the loss of property and life from fires in Jakarta. Loss of life from environmental hazards is increased when people knowingly or unknowingly settle in risk-prone areas (flood plains, seismic fault lines, unstable slopes). Uncontrolled residential and agricultural development of steep slopes south of Jakarta contributed to erosion, with its downstream effects of river siltation, flash flooding, and reduced agricultural productivity. If one result of global warming is a rise in the average sea level, then portions of cities like Accra (the beachfront areas) and Jakarta (low-lying North Jakarta) will face an increased risk of flooding and possible permanent inundation.

Interaction Between Urban Development and the Environment

A3.13   Environmental conditions are often powerful forces that create limits and opportunities for urban development. Similarly, the various individual and collective human activities that contribute to urban development have numerous positive and negative environmental consequences. This section includes examples that illustrate important development-environment interactions. It also presents the case for concern about the environmental shadow that cities cast on the hinterland, using the case of hydropower development for Accra as an illustration.

How environmental factors shape urban development

A3.14   Historically, the initial location and form of each of the case study cities was largely determined by aspects of the natural environment. Accra began in the 16th century as a collection of coastal villages that grew because of their strategic location vis 'a vis natural resources. Fishing constituted the main local economic activity, with substantial trading in ivory, gold, beads and, later, slaves. Jakarta was founded around 1300, and its initial location was also influenced by proximity to resources as well as the ocean. Natural factors (considerable flooding and harbor siltation during the 18th and 19th centuries) caused the Dutch to relocate government buildings to slightly higher ground, an area that is now the city center (Merdeka Square). The first historical references to the Katowice area date from the 12th century and refer to silver ore mining; ironworks went into operation during the 15th century. The spatial design of Katowice has been very much determined by its resource base, with city centers in the upper silesian industrial region being dominated by mines and related industries and wastes. São Paulo was founded in 1554 as an alternative to the hot climate along the coast. For three centuries, it was difficult to access and population growth was slow; the city expanded rapidly beginning only during the first decades of this century, with the availability of cheap hydropower resources and the influx of educated European immigrants. Singrauli is the site of India's largest coal reserves; their exploitation in the 1970s, together with the development of the power industry, led to rapid growth. Tianjin owes much of its economic growth to its favorable location and its resource endowment; it is linked with the three most economically powerful regions of the country and local resources (petroleum, salt, and metallic and other minerals) have been crucial to the creation and growth of several key activities. Since the founding of Carthage as a center of the Punic commercial empire, Tunis has benefited from its strategic maritime location and as a trading gateway to the Mahgreb, subSaharan Africa, and the Middle East.

A3.15   Currently, environmental variables are still affecting the development opportunities for these cities. With low population density and few topographical barriers, Accra's growth is less constrained than the other cities'. Several environmental factors limit development in certain areas: (a) the carrying capacity of Korle Lagoon is being exceeded so new sewage disposal options must be considered; (b) a lack of geologically sound open sites in the city means that new solid waste disposal alternatives must be developed beyond the current in-town options; and (c) shoreline erosion has required the construction of revetments, groins, and gabions or has resulted in the loss of coastal properties. Public officials in Jakarta have consciously steered development away from the southern part of Jabotabek, toward the east and west, to protect the sensitive watershed located there. Also, flooding continues to damage settlements, infrastructure, and commerce in the northern part of the city, necessitating preventive investments in flood control and incurring cleanup costs. The prevalent winds and meteorological conditions in Katowice cause its residents to be exposed to high levels of air pollutants from the region, neighboring countries, and the city's own activities, resulting in health and productivity losses. São Paulo's airshed is subject to frequent inversions, leading to similar costs. Also, the metropolitan area must now grapple with how to protect a critical water supply catchment area that is inhabited by over half a million people. Thus, environmental conditions continue to shape the course and nature of development in these cities.

The impact of urban development on the immediate environment

A3.16   More often than not the human activities that contribute to a city's development have important consequences for environmental quality in the region. In the case study cities, these interactions have been most significant in the following categories: demographics, water management, sanitation, waste management, energy, transportation, housing, mining, and health care. Key interactions in each of these categories are presented below.

A3.17   Perhaps the most significant source of environmental change in urban regions is migratory and natural **population growth.** São Paulo provides a useful illustration of this point. Rapid population growth in the metropolitan region has had two streams of environmental impacts. First, urbanization and industrialization have been intertwined in the São Paulo metropolitan region's economic development. Federal policies of import substitution and industrialization attracted and relied on a large, skilled labor force. The growth of this population helped build and expand a number of industries in and around the region that emit a range of pollutants, for example, automobile manufacture, electrical appliances, steel, petrochemicals, and fertilizers. The second set of impacts stem from the resource requirements of the growing number of city dwellers themselves. The component of the population that is born in the city—accounting for almost 40 percent of population growth in the São Paulo metropolitan region—places a demand on existing infrastructure (water, sanitation, health, waste management, transport) while the migratory component often creates a demand for new services in the periphery. Often environmental services and infrastructure cannot be adequately provided by the public sector and the substitutes provided by the private/ informal sectors may not be ecologically sound. These dynamics of population growth underlie many of the worsening interactions that are described below. On the more positive side, São Paulo's urbanization has reduced pressure on rural resources and possibly lessened the degree of human infringement on ecologically fragile lands.

A3.18   Evidence suggests that **family planning** (or its absence) can have an important effect on such rapid population growth. In Accra, with one of the most poorly rated family planning programs in subSaharan Africa, 93 percent of married women know about contraception methods but only 1.5 percent use modern techniques because of problems of access and affordability. However, the stakes are high: if fertility is not reduced from six to three children per woman, the Accra metropolitan authority's population will stand at 5.9 million in 2015, instead of 4.2 million. The 40 percent difference has significant implications for the need to maintain and supply key environmental services and infrastructure, energy, transport, low-risk land, and acceptable housing. Jakarta, Katowice, and São Paulo benefit from more successful birth control practices (with respective contraceptive prevalence rates of 54 percent, 80 percent, and 74 percent). Still, the population of each of these cities is growing faster than the national average; this is explained by an important natural rate of increase that is supplemented by a contribution from migration. For example, in Tianjin, with an effective family planning program, population increases are driven by a net migration rate of 4.2 percent.

A3.19   **Water supply and distribution** are environmental services; how they are provided has had important environmental effects. In Accra and Jakarta, the supply of piped water to low income neighborhoods is inadequate, forcing many poor people to seek costly and often unsanitary alternatives.[2] In most of the cities, industrial growth coupled with inadequate waste treatment and the absence of conservation measures is having a range of environmental impacts: (a) overexploitation and contamination of groundwater reserves in Jakarta, Katowice, and Tianjin and contamination of surface water in Singrauli; (b) water shortages for residential and industrial consumers in Katowice, São Paulo, and Tianjin; (c) growing competition for water between farmers and urban consumers in the Jabotabek region; and (d) increasing costs of additional increments of water supply, as in Jakarta, São Paulo, and Tianjin. Also, problems with water management in one area can affect another: in Jakarta, land subsidence exacerbated by overuse of the aquifer is threatening some of the key flood control works in the northern part of the city. On the positive side, reduced groundwater extraction and artificial recharge in Tianjin have significantly reduced land subsidence and have resulted in a 9.6 m rise in the water table, and investments in interbasin transfers as well as sanitation systems in the Medjerda valley have protected the quality of Tunis' drinking water. So, the way that water is managed for urban development can have important environmental consequences, with associated impacts on human health and productivity.

A3.20   **Sanitation,** including wastewater treatment, is an important environmental service that is closely linked to water management. The key conclusions are as follows:

- In all of the cities, a significant part of water pollution is directly caused by **poor**

---

2. In the slum areas of Accra where water is frequently purchased and/or supply is irregular, daily per capita consumption is about 60 liters, compared to 100–120 liters for middle-income neighborhoods, and 120-200 liters for wealthy areas (Ghana Water and Sewerage Corporation, *Five Year Rehabilitation and Development Plan,* Accra: GWSC, 1986, pp. D3 and F-10, and E.Y.S. Engmann, *Urban Utilities and Municipal Services,* Accra: UNCHS, pp. 62–68). So in poor communities water is often conveyed from untreated sources in open buckets to households where it may be stored in drums, resulting in many opportunities for contamination. In Jakarta, only 60 percent of the population is served by the treated drinking water supply system. In the slums, water is priced at an equivalent of $1.50-5.20/m3, while the average tariff for piped water to connected households is $0.10-0.50/m3 (Laszlo Lovei and D. Whittington "Rent Seeking in Water Supply," *World Bank Infrastructure and Urban Department Discussion Paper No. 85,* September 1991, p. 7). In addition, 58 percent of water from handcarts shows signs of fecal coliform contamination (Edwardi Budirahardjo and Charles Surjadi, "Environmental and Health Problems in Jakarta," paper presented to the Stockholm Environment Institute Workshop on Urban Household Environment, June 17-21, 1991, p. 8).

management of the sanitation system. In Accra, outfall from the poorly functioning central sewage system contaminates the beaches; poor system coverage results in serious lagoon and stream pollution, as well as soil contamination from open defecation in slum and periurban areas. In Jakarta, where the central system reaches less than 1 percent of the population, the aquifer is being gradually contaminated by seepage from poorly maintained septic tanks. In Katowice, only one quarter of municipal sewage receives proper treatment; consequently, organic substances constitute an important part of the surface water pollution load. In the São Paulo metropolitan region, only 40 percent of collected sewage receives some sort of treatment. Consequently, a recent analysis of 15 years of water quality data concludes that organic waste from households is the worst polluter of key water bodies. Similar problems exist in Tianjin, where the treatment rate is 45 percent.

- Access to and affordability of adequate sanitation is **a problem for the poor**, especially in the lower-income cities. In the poor areas of Accra, the most common forms of human waste disposal are pit, pan, and bucket latrines and open defecation. There are slums in North Jakarta where more than half of the children younger than age five used sewers, ditches, and open spaces, and half of the overall population did not live in facilities with a private toilet. In Tianjin, old neighborhoods and slums rely on public latrines without proper flushing, sewage connections, or capacity.

- One result of this combination of poor management and a low level of service to the poor is that **inadequate sanitation can have negative health effects.** In Jakarta, the neighborhoods with high levels of BOD in their water systems (due, in large part, to inadequate human waste disposal) have higher incidences of waterborne diseases. This is especially true in the poor areas in the north of the city.[3] Tianjin's lack of hygiene linked to poor sewage is suspected of contributing the high incidence of gastrointestinal diseases in the municipality.

So, poor sanitation is an environmental problem that has managerial, equity, and health dimensions.

A3.21   As with sanitation, inadequate **municipal and industrial solid waste disposal** creates a range of environmental problems. The situations for municipal and industrial wastes are presented separately. Although all of the cities have generally well-functioning **municipal solid waste** (MSW)-collection services (see following section on environmental management), MSW disposal is generally not well handled. In Jakarta, considerable amounts of waste are disposed of in an uncontrolled way by being buried, burnt, thrown on open land, or dumped in drains, canals, and rivers. The situation is exacerbated in slums where only 37 percent of households can make use of garbage-collection containers. As for the official disposal system, the three aging landfill sites suffer from some leaching that pollutes the aquifer, and methane gas generated by biochemical degradation may

---

3. This conclusion comes from analysis of maps that depict the number of waterborne diseases contracted over a three-year period and BOD measurements throughout the Jakarta water supply system.

constitute an explosion risk. None of the 45 dump sites in the Katowice voivodeship employ sanitary landfill practices; their environmental impacts have not been assessed but could be expected to be similar to those in Jakarta. In São Paulo, the main environmental problems associated with poor MSW disposal are: (a) air pollution from open burning of undisposed solid waste[4]; (b) groundwater contamination; (c) surface water pollution; and (d) soil contamination. In Tunis, there are two unsanitary landfills and 17 illegal dumps, none with separation of municipal and hospital wastes. Only Tianjin has good waste-disposal practices, with 18 percent of MSW transformed into high-quality compost, 51 percent to low-quality compost, 29 percent disposed of in sanitary landfills, and only 2 percent openly dumped.

A3.22   In the more developed cities, improper disposal of **industrial and hazardous wastes** is an important environmental problem that affects air, water, and land quality. In Jakarta's seven major rivers, 23 percent–67 percent of chemical oxygen demand is attributed to industrial pollutants. In Katowice, 78 percent of industrial solid wastes are dumped on the surface, and there are no special facilities for treating hazardous wastes. As mentioned in the Katowice summary, the majority of air, water, and land pollutants come from industrial sources. In São Paulo and Tianjin, where there have been relatively effective programs for industrial pollution control, environmental risks stem from heavy metals in the air, water, and soil because of the lack of a hazardous waste treatment program (in São Paulo, 20 percent—13 percent in Tianjin— of industrial solid waste is considered to be hazardous). An important aspect of the waste problem is that, especially in the lower-income cities, much of it originates from small-scale and cottage industries. In Accra, many small workshops and garages discharge their untreated wastes directly into drains that pollute the lagoon. In Jakarta, an estimated 75 percent of the 4,000 polluting industries in the metropolitan area are small-scale producers of, for example, wood products, electronics, pesticides, batteries, electroplating, paints, ceramics, textiles, and tanneries. These waste generators constitute a particularly difficult problem because they are numerous and dispersed, making them hard to regulate, with the perpetrators hard to educate and involve in waste treatment programs.

A3.23   Each of the cities illustrates a different aspect of the environmental dimension of **urban energy consumption**. In Accra, the combustion of biomass fuels (charcoal and wood) in households may result in serious levels of **indoor air pollution**.[5] In Jakarta, cutting wood as a source of urban energy was an important cause of **periurban deforestation** (along with the demand for construction and furniture materials). This problem has been significantly reduced as city households have shifted to using kerosene and LPG (liquified petroleum gas) as their primary cooking fuels. As with many cities, Jakarta has undergone an energy transition from biomass to fossil fuels, and the structure of its energy-linked environmental problems has shifted accordingly. In Katowice and Tianjin, **dependence on coal** as the primary source of energy for power generation and household heating has resulted in worsened air quality; one fifth of all CO emissions in the voivodeship come solely from coal combustion for electricity generation; in Tianjin, 65 percent of total suspended particulates

---

4. Eighteen percent of suspended particulate matter measured in the São Paulo metropolitan region comes from open fires (CETESB *Relatorio de qualidade do ar no Estado de São Paulo*, São Paulo: Author, 1990).

5. This has yet to be proven in Accra. Indoor air quality is being measured by the University of Ghana (Legon) in a study financed by the Stockholm Environment Institute. These measurements will be available in 1993. Evidence from other areas of the world where households burn biomass indoors indicates that there is an indoor air pollution problem (Kirk Smith, *Biofuels, Air Pollution and Health: A Global Review*, New York: Plenum Press, 1987).

come from enterprises that generate power, raise steam, and heat water. In the extreme case of Singrauli, with 6,500 MW of installed capacity, pollution from coal-fired power plants has had a serious impact on the air and water quality, as well as natural ecosystems. In São Paulo, **changes in the hydrological regime to supply hydropower** led to serious water pollution problems. To have adequate water for energy production at the hydro station in Cubatao, the Tiete and Pinheiros rivers were reversed toward the Billings reservoir; the reversal brought pollution from the rivers to the reservoir, accounting for much of its degraded condition. As of mid-1993, this practice has stopped but now there are concerns about adequate reservoir capacity.

A3.24   The nature of urban **transportation and telecommunications** systems also has important environmental consequences. In most of the cities, the motorized fleet is growing at a faster rate than the population or the road capacity: in Jakarta, the number of motor vehicles has increased 10 percent–13 percent per annum in recent years; population road surface has expanded by 3 percent, and population has increased by 2.4 percent. Consequently, air pollution from mobile sources has become a growing problem. One particularly harmful aspect of this growth is the use of leaded fuel in all of the cities except São Paulo. A recent study of Bangkok concluded that ingestion of fuel-based lead in the air, water and food was the city's top environmental health problem.[6] Another health-related problem associated with this uneven growth is the increasing number of traffic injuries and fatalities in all of the cities. Tianjin and Tunis constitute two exceptions to the growth scenario: in Tianjin, despite an average annual growth of 10 percent in motor vehicle traffic, 90 percent of passenger trips are by bicycle; in Tunis, the growth in the number of households with an automobile is expected to slow from 2 percent annually (between 1985 and 1996) to 1.4 percent (1996–2001). Both cities possess well-functioning transportation systems that provide commuters with a variety of substitutes for automobile travel.

A3.25   Telecommunications are not very well developed in the seven cities; this has environmental consequences. For example, Katowice has one telephone per 14.5 inhabitants compared with the national average of one per eight residents. In São Paulo, there are still more cars (2.4 million) than telephone terminals (1.9 million) in the metropolitan region. Although 20 percent of households in Tunis have telephone service, compared with a national average of 9 percent, the figure is still low. A possible environmental impact of an underdeveloped urban communications system is increased air pollution from the greater vehicle use and congestion associated with reliance on vehicles, instead of telecommunications, to exchange information.

A3.26   The variables that link **housing** and environmental quality appear to be density, location, and quality of construction. **Crowding** can worsen existing environmental problems in human settlements. Accra's high occupancy rate of 4.4 persons per room in slums like James Town puts heavy pressures on shared facilities like kitchens, toilets, and bathing areas; these areas often have poor drainage so water accumulates, providing a breeding ground for mosquitoes. In São Paulo, crowding has been associated with an increase in communicable diseases. Residential **location** can increase exposure to environmental risks. Low-quality housing that is built on illegally developed land in the earthquake-prone areas of Accra and Tianjin, the flood zones of Jakarta and Tunis, or the fragile hillsides of São Paulo are vulnerable to natural hazards. The residents of apartment buildings

---

6. See USAID/US EPA, *Ranking Environmental Health Risks in Bangkok, Thailand*, Washington, DC: USAID Office of Housing and Urban Programs, 1990.

and worker housing that have been built near factories, power plants, and waste dumps in Katowice and Tianjin are exposed to high levels of air, water, and soil pollutants. In Singrauli, 36 percent of houses are located in unhealthy areas and, in 34 percent of the sites, other dangers exist. Substandard **construction** can also be a source of environmental ills. In São Paulo, environmental health problems linked to poor quality housing include: (a) bronchial illness, colds, influenza, and pneumonia from draughts, dampness, and lack of ventilation; (b) diarrhea and dehydration from inadequate plumbing; (c) bites and the transmission of disease from rats, ticks, spiders, and fleas; and (d) diarrhea, dehydration, worms, and skin diseases from a lack of sanitation facilities.

A3.27   **Mining** is a source of environmental degradation in five of the seven cities. In Accra and São Paulo, the damage is localized. The extraction of clay, sand, and gravel has destroyed surface vegetation and created noise and dust pollution in particular areas of Accra. Sand extraction has adversely affected streambeds, river banks, and water quality in São Paulo, and stone quarries have caused localized noise, vibration, and air pollution problems. In Katowice, mining has produced extensive environmental problems. In addition to mining's contributions to water pollution and solid waste, 25 percent of mined areas suffer from subsidence that annually lead to 8,000 cases of damage to the sewer system, replacement of 800 km of pipelines, and disruption of 400 km of riverbeds. Coal mining in Singrauli is the principal cause of degradation of the local forests and agricultural and drainage systems and has exacerbated air pollution and water-related problems. In the hills surrounding Tunis, poorly regulated quarries contribute to hillside erosion, loss of vegetative cover, dust, and vibrations.

A3.28   Many of these interactions are manifested in the **health and health care systems** of the case study cities. The key observation is that there is a strong link between environmental and health problems in all of the cities:

- Thirteen of the 16 significant diseases that are reported in Accra are associated with poor housing and ventilation, an unsanitary environment, contaminated drinking water, poor drainage, and lack of facilities for waste disposal.

- In Jakarta, diarrhea is correlated with poor drinking water and toilet facilities, the infestation of flies in living quarters, and household proximity to litter. Acute respiratory infection is linked to overcrowding, unventilated construction, insufficient light, indoor air pollution from smoking and cooking, and ambient air pollution. Dengue fever and filariasis are caused by mosquitoes that breed in stagnant pools of water that remain undrained at the end of the rainy season.

- Declining life expectancy in Katowice has been a function of higher rates of cardiovascular diseases, cancer, and digestive tract illnesses. This is consistent with high levels of exposure to carcinogens, heavy contamination of the food supply with industrial effluents, and exposure to air pollutants capable of stressing the cardiorespiratory system;

- Environment-related problems are the leading causes of infant mortality in São Paulo—respiratory conditions and intestinal infections account for nearly half of all infant deaths. In adult morbidity, tuberculosis and cerebrospinal meningitis have been linked to overcrowding, substandard housing, and poor ventilation, and the degree of respiratory ill health in children has been correlated with level of air pollution.

- In Singrauli, 26 percent of residents perceive discomfort from chimney factories, 19 percent mention link health problems to the workplace, and 15 percent regard road traffic as dangerous.

- For Tianjin, the highest occurrences of environmental diseases (lung cancer, infant mortality, tuberculosis, and cervical cancer) are linked to two possible pathological factors: atmospheric pollution or unhealthy workplace conditions, or a combination of both.

- Mortality in Tunis is caused less by infectious diseases and increasingly by cardiovascular and respiratory ailments. This transition is being accelerated by exposure to urban pollutants, as well as changes in lifestyle.

A3.29   These problems are often worse for the poor, who have the lowest access rate to (and ability to pay for) formal health care. For example, in São Paulo the central subregion had 3.1 hospital beds per 1,000 inhabitants and the poorest peripheral areas had 0.4 beds; of the 1,351 outpatient clinics in the São Paulo metropolitan region, 987 (73 %) were located in the central subregion and only eight (0.6%) were in the northern subregion, one of the poorest. The problems can also result in large economic losses. In the Katowice voivodeship, 36.7 million productive days are lost due to illness, equivalent to 150 hours annually per worker. In 1988, 87 percent of these compensable occupational diseases were environment related (40 percent occupational deafness, 30 percent pneumoconiosis, 10 percent lead poisoning, and 7 percent vibration syndrome). In Ghana, 70 percent of health care costs have been attributed to environment-related diseases.[7]

The impact of urban development on rural areas

A3.30   Urban areas transform but rarely produce natural resources that come from elsewhere—the hinterland, far-flung regions of the country, or overseas. The way that this demand is met can have serious environmental consequences in areas that are located far from the city. This point is illustrated with a brief example of hydropower development for Accra and is extrapolated to cover other resources. The environmental profile of Singrauli provides a more extensive and complicated picture of this "urban shadow" effect.

A3.31   In the Accra metropolitan area, the main consumer of electricity is the Volta Aluminum Company, a transnational company that processes aluminum from imported alumina. The power is purchased from the Volta River Authority's national grid, which transmits electricity from two hydroelectric power stations. These are located about 80 km from Accra, at Akosombo and Kpong in the eastern region of the country. Both dams were built on the Volta River.

A3.32   On the negative side, the formation of Lake Volta behind Akosombo dam displaced about 80,000 people in 700 villages. Manatee that used to be spotted before the formation of the lake have not been seen since. The lake has provided an ideal environment for the proliferation of snails

---

7. This estimate takes account of lost work hours and the cost of resources such as doctors, nurses, technicians, administration, equipment, and drugs (F.J. Convery and K.A. Tutu, *Evaluating the Costs of Environmental Degradation in Ghana*, Report to the Environmental Protection Council/World Bank, 1990).

that transmit schistosomiasis; there have been severe outbreaks among fishermen along the lake. Prawn and clam catches were an important economic activity for settlements along the river but have been substantially reduced since the construction of the dam at Kpong.

A3.33   More positively, the lake created a navigable channel of 463 km, thus enabling transport of goods to and from the north of the country. Fish catches rose dramatically, reaching 40,000 tons by 1970, a figure that far exceeded predicted levels. A number of breeding grounds of the black fly, the vector of onchocerciasis (river blindness) were flooded and eliminated. The lake has also increased the potential for irrigated agriculture as well as opportunities for developing recreational and tourist facilities.[8]

A3.34   Similar cases of bad and good rural environmental impacts from urban development exist. A less-than-comprehensive list would include:

- Reduced pressure on fragile rural ecosystems when underemployed peasants migrate to cities.

- Similar environmental consequences to the Accra hydropower case when dams and other waterworks are constructed to supply urban residential and industrial consumers with water.

- Ecological degradation and the displacement of settlements from mining to supply mineral resources for urban industries and coal for power generation to meet urban demand for electricity (e.g., Singrauli).

- Periurban deforestation to meet commercialized urban demand for wood fuels and rural deforestation to supply construction timber.

Although these effects may occur far from the city, they probably would not occur or would not be as pronounced without the impetus of urban development.

The Institutional Setting for Environmental Management

A3.35   Environmental problems and the opportunities for managing them exist within contexts unique to each city but with common characteristics. The central elements that shape the institutional setting for environmental management are: (a) the key actors in the public and private sectors whose motives and mandates significantly affect the urban environment; (b) the management functions that can be or are used to address environmental issues in cities, including instruments of intervention and mechanisms for coordination; and (c) the existing constraints and initiatives that affect efforts to manage environmental problems in cities.

Key actors

A3.36   Initially, actors can be divided between those in the public and private sectors. In the public sector, there are central government agencies (ministries and special bodies), regional

---

8. *Republic of Ghana Institutional Capacities for Assessing Impacts and Trade-offs of Large Hydro-dams: Case Study of the Volta Hydropower Project*, Accra: Ministry of Fuel and Power, 1989.

government institutions (agencies and special bodies), and local government departments; individual players (politicians and officials) are also represented at each of these levels of government. The private sector, as broadly defined in this analysis, includes private and informal sector enterprises, community groups, nongovernmental organizations (NGOs), and the media. The existence and agendas of community organizations and NGOs are taken as proxies for the desires (but not necessarily the actions) of individual households and neighborhoods. An alternative would be to directly assess the role of individuals, families, and communities; however, the research did not encompass this level of disaggregation.[9] The influence of bilateral and multilateral aid agencies is reflected in the activities of the actors that they support (public and/or private) and in the paragraphs on constraints and initiatives. The role of the academic community is covered in the section on management functions that deals with education, training and research.

A3.37   In the public sector, each of the cities is embedded in a different set of political and fiscal arrangements that affect environmental management; these are briefly described in the summaries of the environmental profiles provided in Volume 2. Accra is part of a political system characterized by a strong central government, a weaker authority known as the Greater Accra Region, and a metropolitan authority that is in the process of expanding its mandate. Jakarta also operates with a strong national government but has a metropolitan structure that is divided between two relatively strong provincial governments, and a weaker set of local governments. Although the institutional arrangements affecting Katowice have been evolving over the past three years, it appears to be in a situation where there are strong central government actors, voivodeship-level authorities that are asserting political autonomy but do not yet have financial resources, and weaker local bodies. In São Paulo, the 1988 constitution weakened the federal and metropolitan levels of government while strengthening the political and fiscal authority of state and municipal governments. Land planning, zoning, infrastructure development, and environmental protection are complicated in Singrauli because they are in the hands of Special Area District Authorities in two separate states (Uttar Pradesh and Madhya Pradesh). Urban management in Tianjin is facilitated as the Tianjin municipal government is responsible for direct administration of the city proper as well as the surrounding counties and has provincial status in the national political system. Greater Tunis is administered by three governorates (Ben Arous, Ariana, and Tunis), though *de facto* power is shared with certain national ministries. Table A3.1 provides a summary matrix of environmental responsibilities by level of government.

A3.38   In all cases, at the **central** level of government, there is a range of up to a dozen national ministries that make rules, wield power, and allocate funds that affect urban environmental management. The most important ministries are those that concern local government, the environment, public works, planning, finance, industry, health, and transportation. There are also special bodies that can be important in a particular urban sector or because of their cross-sectoral nature. For example, the Ghana Water Supply and Sewerage Corporation is the key actor for managing water and sanitation in Accra, the Brazilian Institute of the Environment and Renewable Natural Resources sets or approves federal standards for water and air quality that affect São Paulo, and the Central Mine

---

9. To make up for this knowledge gap, the Stockholm Environment Institute is undertaking a household environmental study in three of the four cities (Accra, Jakarta, and São Paulo). It includes both a random sample survey of about 1,000 households in each city and physical measurements of environmental quality at the residential level (indoor air quality, water quality, sanitation, and presence of insects and rodents) in a subsample of about 200 households per city. Analyzed results from this inquiry should be available by the end of 1993.

Table A3.1. Urban environmental management matrix

Level	Laws, regulations & responsibilties							
CENTRAL GOVERNMENT	Policy	Air	Water	Sani-tation	SWM	Drain-age	Trans-port	Ind. Poll.
Urban Ministry	A,S							
Environmental Ministry/Council	all	A,TI, K, S	A,J,K, S,TI					A,J,K, S,TU
Planning Ministry	J							
Other Ministry	K		J	J	J	J	SP	A,J,K
Special Body	S	S,SP	A,J,S, SP,TU	A,TU		A,J,S,TU	A,S,TU	J,S,SP
REGIONAL GOVERNMENT								
Executive	A,J	J	J,TI	J	J		J	TI
Environmental Agency	J,K	K,SP	K,SP					K,SP,T,I
Planning Agency							S	
Other Agency	TI		J	J,TI	J,TI,TU	J,TI	J,K,SP,TI	J,SP
Special Body	S	J,SP	S,SP	SP		S,SP	TU	SP
LOCAL GOVERNMENT								
Executive	A							
Environmental Department				J				
Planning Department								
Other Department				SP	all		A,K	
Special Body				SP		S		
PRIVATE SECTOR			J,S	A,S	A,J,S, SP		J,S,TU	J,S
NGOs/ COMMUNITY					J,S	J		
ACADEMIA								

A = Accra; J = Jakarta; K = Katowice; S = Singrauli; SP = São Paulo; TI = Tianjin; TU = Tunis; all = all cities

Table A3.1 (continued). Urban environmental management matrix

Level	Managerial instruments					
CENTRAL GOVERNMENT	Econ. Fiscal	Planning	EIA	Monitoring	Education/ Training	Coord.
Urban Ministry	J	J,S				S
Environmental Ministry/Council	T,I	A,K,S, SP	A,J,S,TU	TU		A,SP
Planning Ministry	J	A,J,K,SP				J
Other Ministry	A,J,K				all	
Special Body	S	S	J	AS		J
REGIONAL GOVERNMENT						
Executive						
Environmental Agency	SP,TI	K,SP	SP,TI	K,SP,TI	TI	K,SP,TI
Planning Agency		J				
Other Agency		TI			J,SP	TI
Special Body	S,SP	S		J,S		J
LOCAL GOVERNMENT						
Executive		SP				A
Environmental Department						
Planning Department						SP
Other Department					SP	K
Special Body						
PRIVATE SECTOR			A,J	A,J		
NGOs/ COMMUNITY					all	
ACADEMIA			A	J,K	A,J,K,SP	

Planning and Design Institute has broad responsibility for mine development and environmental management in Singrauli.

A3.39   **Regionally**, the arrangements differ more from city to city. In Accra, the Regional Authority appears to be little more than an institutional mechanism for interpreting and implementing national programs and policies. In Jakarta, the province of DKI Jakarta manages the capital city, and the province of West Java is responsible for the areas of the metropolis outside of the central city. Both play a major role in determining local environmental policy, implementing programs, and managing funds. Many of the key environmental decisions are made and executed at the voivodeship level in Katowice, including those concerning environmental and industrial policy. In São Paulo, the state government plays a critical role in environmental regulation, water supply and sanitation, and industrial pollution control. For Tianjin, the provincial authority and the municipal government are one and the same. In Tunis, the Regional Councils, presided by the governors of the three governorates that comprise Greater Tunis, have budgetary authority.

A3.40   The environmental roles of **local** authorities also differ widely between the cities. At the most limited end of the scale, the Accra Metropolitan Authority has been primarily responsible for solid waste management (SWM). A broader range of responsibilities are handled in different ways by the other cities. In Jabotabek (the Jakarta metropolitan area), authorities from different cities are jointly responsible with agencies of the provincial governments for SWM, sanitation, local roads, small industries, data collection, and environmental education. In Katowice, the municipalities handle SWM, health care, housing, land use planning, communications, and public transportation. The municipal authorities in the São Paulo metropolitan region are responsible for SWM, noise pollution control, parks and recreation, education, health, public transportation, and zoning. The common denominator for these and other cities around the world is that they are involved in some manner with the collection and disposal of solid waste. Local District Assemblies in Singrauli control development credits, but much of the authority for planning and implementation rests with the state-level Special Area District Authorities. The Tianjin metropolitan government manages SWM, roads, and drainage, but other revenue-earning services such as housing, water, and public transport are provided by public sector companies. In Greater Tunis, municipalities are responsible for the collection and transport of solid waste, street cleaning, maintenance of drains, and provision of green space.

A3.41   **Local politicians** can play a crucial role in mobilizing resources to achieve environmental goals although, more often than not, they avoid persistent environmental problems and solutions that have long-term payoffs. The former chairman of the Accra metropolitan authority invested much of his time ensuring the success of a program to clean up the physical appearance of the city through improved solid waste collection and sanitation services. Striking cases of the power of local officials to transform the urban environment exist in cities other than those studied. The former mayor of Tianjin was able to combine his grassroots support with high-level political connections in Beijing to mobilize local and national financial and human resources to invest in a wide range of environmental improvements, for example, slum upgrading, China's largest wastewater treatment plant, massive coal gasification facilities, construction of a series of ring roads and a subway, and a series of investments from an industrial pollution control fund.[10]

---

10. In another oft-cited example, a strong mayor of Curitiba, Brazil, was the driving force that transformed the city into the "ecological capital" of the country through environmentally responsible transport planning, resource recovery, urban design, industrial location and pollution control, preservation of cultural heritage and open space, and public education (Jonas Rabinovitch with J. Leitmann, *Environmental Innovations and Management in Curitiba, Brazil*, UMP Working Paper, No. 1, June 1993).

A3.42   In the private sector, different configurations of **private enterprises** play important environmental roles. Accra and Tunis are characterized by several large corporations that have influence at the national level, and many small-scale polluters. Private firms are also active in the fields of solid waste collection, sanitation, and environmental consulting. Jakarta and São Paulo have a wide range of private industries that are involved, to varying degrees, in waste management and pollution control. Private actors are also involved in toll road operations, industrial estate development, municipal SWM, and environmental consulting. The overwhelming majority of industrial and manufacturing firms in Katowice and Tianjin are still state owned, so there is little private enterprise to speak of. Singrauli represents a middle ground where the key polluting firms are a mix of state enterprise (e.g., the National Thermal Power Corporation, National Coalfields Ltd., Uttar Pradesh State Electricity Board) and private concerns (e.g., Kanoria Chemicals and Hindalco Aluminum Ltd.).

A3.43   In several of the cities, **community organizations** play an important role in providing environmental services that are not adequately supplied by the state. In Accra, community groups have been involved in operating basic sanitation services, conducting neighborhood and stream cleanup campaigns, and promoting environmental awareness. In Jakarta, neighborhood organizations have been very active in solid waste collection and environmental education. São Paulo represents a successful case of direct household involvement in environmental management: SWM collection is facilitated because 70 percent of residential solid waste is put out for collection already packed in plastic bags, compared to 30 percent in Rio. Community groups in the São Paulo metropolitan region have also played an important role in environmental monitoring by notifying the state environmental protection company about industrial polluters.

A3.44   In all of the cities, **NGOs** with an environmental focus exist, but they have different objectives, levels of influence, and audiences. In Accra, there are indigenous NGOs and local affiliates of international groups; they tend to be either those concerned with natural resource issues or those that focus on environmental education and health. There are about 30 NGOs with an environmental focus operating in Jakarta; they are active in a range of issues from appropriate technology to land tenure, often in low-income communities. In Katowice, and throughout Poland, strong NGOs emerged as a tolerated outlet for political dissent during the communist era; they are actively involved in the development and implementation of environmental, industrial, and health care policies. In São Paulo, some nongovernmental groups focus on housing and poverty issues, while others tend to reflect the priority interests of the well-off, for example, green space, forest preservation, and protective zoning. NGO activism in Singrauli has focused on defending the interests of "environmental refugees" whose lands were expropriated for mining and power development. In Tunis and Tianjin, there is little NGO activity not linked to the official political structure, except for professional associations that seek to promote civil awareness of environmental issues.

A3.45   Finally, the **media** play a variable role that is usually commensurate with the degree of political freedom in the country. In countries with more authoritarian governments (China, Ghana, and Indonesia), the media are often reluctant to investigate and draw attention to polluters, their victims, and government shortcomings. In states with more (or relatively newfound) freedom (Brazil, India, Poland, and Tunisia), there is more evidence of investigative environmental journalism in cities. The press in the cities of the Katowice voivodeship have been important organs for NGOs and have publicized what were once secret statistics on environmental degradation. In São Paulo, the media regularly carry stories on particular environmental problems such as congestion, air and water pollution, and hazardous wastes, and sometimes take an active role in problem solving.[11]

Management functions

A3.46   As defined here, management functions consist of the policy and other instruments that actors can wield to affect environmental quality and the mechanisms through which they work to make and coordinate environment-oriented decisions. The instruments that have been reviewed in the case study cities fall in the following categories: legislative and regulatory; planning and monitoring; economic incentives and direct investment; education, training ,and research; and promotion and protest. The actors who wield these tools are listed in Table A3-1. The decision-oriented variables that were reviewed include: (a) the role of public participation in environmental management; (b) issues of intersectoral and intergovernmental coordination; and (c) relations between the public and private sectors.

A3.47   **Instruments.** The most prevalent tool for environmental management that affects city is that of **legislation and regulation**. The sophistication and effectiveness of this tool runs the range from low in Accra to reasonably high in São Paulo and Tianjin. In Ghana, there are few environmental standards and an incomplete set of environmental laws; lack of enforcement is a pervasive problem in both Ghana and Tunisia. An environmental impact assessment (EIA) process is being designed and selectively implemented in both countries. In Indonesia and India, national legislation is reasonably comprehensive and supplemented by provincial regulations; again, enforcement is weak. New air, water, and industrial standards were issued in 1991, and all industries were subject to an EIA process as of June 1992. Poland has a comprehensive set of environmental laws and standards for the range of environmental media, including noise pollution; however, they are unevenly observed and enforced. Brazil and China also have sophisticated sets of environmental legislation, regulations, and standards; in many instances, these have been made more stringent by the state or provincial-level government. In the São Paulo metropolitan region, there has been more success in enforcing particular control measures such as those affecting industrial air and water emissions, transportation, and fuel quality.

A3.48   **Planning** has generally not been an effective environmental tool in the cities, although **monitoring** varies according to the city's level of economic and human resource development. In the Accra metropolitan authority, planning has made its most visible mark in the contrast between the city of Accra (unplanned and relatively unmanaged environmental problems) and the port of Tema (a planned community with reasonably good environmental services and infrastructure). Monitoring is irregular, except for the case of water quality, which is routinely measured. In both Jabotabek and DKI Jakarta, planning has been seriously adopted as a policy instrument[12] and, as mentioned, has been effective in guiding land development away from environmentally sensitive areas. Monitoring is limited for air pollution and industrial emissions but is fairly extensive for water quality. The

---

11. For example, a popular radio station (Radio Eldorado) has initiated a campaign to clean up the Tiete River that has attracted a large amount of community and official support.

12. Four key plans have affected urban environmental developments in the metropolis: the Jakarta Metropolitan Development Plan (1980), the Jakarta Structure Plan (for the 1985-2005 period), the Botabek Urban Development Project (1985), and the Provincial Five Year Plan (for both provinces).

Katowice voivodeship has only recently been given the authority to plan and has produced documents for attaining environmental objectives and industrial restructuring, so it is too early to evaluate the effectiveness of this tool. Monitoring is quite extensive, with regular measurements of air, water, and soil quality and industrial pollutants. São Paulo has been unable to undertake much planning at the metropolitan level because of difficulties in coordinating 38 independent municipalities but has had more success with zoning at the city level, except in the case of the Guarapiranga reservoir/catchment area. As in Katowice, monitoring is extensive and regular, with implementation being the responsibility of a state agency. The national Town and Country Planning Organization has drafted a regional plan for Singrauli (including the identification of critical environmental zones and priority actions) and is now in the process of preparing a strategic action plan. Environmental planning in Tianjin is based on effective environmental zoning for the city, agricultural areas, and watersheds, along with air, water, and noise quality targets for each zone. Planning has not been an effective instrument in Tunis for preserving green space but has been effective in transportation management.

A3.49   **Economic** policy instruments are generally not used to directly affect the quality of the urban environment; **direct investment** is a more common monetary tool of intervention. Ghana has indirectly affected urban resource consumption through import tariffs on vehicles with large engines and subsidies for LPG cookstoves. It has been more active in mobilizing investment in urban infrastructure and services, often with donor support.[13] The principal area where economic incentives have been used for environmental management in Jakarta has been low land prices and property taxes to encourage industrial development to the east and west of DKI Jakarta. Direct investment has been an essential tool, with government, private, and aid resources being mobilized for transportation, pollution control, industrial development, water supply, sanitation, flood control and institutional development projects and programs. Poland has a comprehensive system of effluent charges and penalties, but they are minuscule and have virtually no impact on emissions.[14] There has been relatively little direct investment in pollution control (though donor support is being mobilized for this purpose); public money has primarily gone for water supply and sanitation. Several underutilized economic instruments exist in the São Paulo metroplitan region: (a) the water and sewerage tariffs have been set at a rate that covers short-run marginal cost, but they are well below the long-run cost of needed investments in interceptors and sewage treatment; (b) user charges are imposed for other environmental services and infrastructure but are based on average rather than marginal costs; and (c) property taxes are based on a technical rather than market value, so they have not been able to serve as a source of sufficient revenues to maintain services and infrastructure. Direct investment has had a much more significant impact on the urban environment, with local, state, national, and donor resources supporting water supply, sewage collection and treatment, industrial pollution control, gasohol, and health care. In Singrauli, a tax of Rs 12-15/ton of coal extracted is levied with half used

---

13. For example, the German government has provided support for the Accra metropolitan authority to invest in reorganizing and improving the city's Waste Management Department. The World Bank has provided two loans for investments in urban infrastructure. A large amount of money was invested to prepare the city to host the 1991 Nonaligned Movement conference, though there is no evidence that environmental criteria were used to guide these investments.

14. Effluent charges in 1987 represented 0.5 percent of the production costs of energy and mining, even though these industries were the worst polluters. In the same year, fines against these enterprises for violating pollution standards reduced their profits by only 0.7 percent on average ("Environment in Eastern Europe: Despair or Hope?" *Transition: The Newsletter about Reforming Economies*, 2(4) World Bank, April 1991, p. 10).

for the mitigation of air, water, and noise pollution. Tianjin employs a range of economic instruments for pollution control (pollution discharge fee, tax incentives for control, other economic incentives) but does not seek to influence resource pricing. Direct investment has also had an enormous impact of environmental quality, for example, the sewage treatment and coal gasification facilities. Tunis benefits from national tariff and tax incentives for industrial pollution control investments.

A3.50   Each city's level of **education, training, and research** concerning the urban environment appears to be correlated with its level of economic development. The poorest city, Accra, has the weakest reliance on this instrument. There are institutions that undertake all three functions, but the activities are often in the stages of early development, underfunded and infrequently pursued. Jakarta has benefited from greater use of this tool for human resource and knowledge development: basic environmental studies are part of the school curriculum; there are regular public awareness campaigns; professional environmental training and research are conducted by several academic institutions; and environmental leadership training is provided at the provincial level for local officials. São Paulo has institutionalized many of these activities in the state's environmental company (CETESB), which undertakes research and training for environmental health, pollution control and prevention, environmental management, monitoring and analysis, and technology transfer. Katowice has the most well-developed set of instruments in this area, with: (a) post-secondary or university departments for air pollution control, environmental engineering, and environmental biology; (b) courses on water purification, sewage treatment, air pollution technology, and industrial pollution control; (c) state research institutes and stations that gather and analyze data on heavy industry, soils, pesticides, food, and occupational health; and (d) an environmental protection course as part of the secondary school curriculum. Tianjin and Tunis are the exceptions to the rule. At the low end of the income scale, Tianjin has municipal and submunicipal programs for urban environmental education using newspapers, TV, special publications, and neighborhood social education, secondary and tertiary training facilities, and research by municipal and academic institutes. At the high end, environmental education in Tunis began only in 1990 via radio and TV, supplemented by NGO activities. Limited urban environmental research is conducted by the university and specialized institutes.

A3.51   **Promotion and protest** are selectively used as instruments to affect environmental management, depending on the political and cultural character of the city. In Accra, with an authoritarian government but a tradition of vocalizing discontent, public protests have been limited, with some complaints about odors from industrial emissions; community organizations and clubs have engaged in more promotional activities such as cleanup campaigns. In Jakarta, with an authoritarian government and a culture that is averse to direct confrontation, there have been low-key, localized protests about visible pollutants (waste water pouring directly from a factory into a river, or exhaust stacks spreading black smoke and dust); promotion has been from the government (such as the awards for the cleanest city, best community and best *kelurahan*) or has been sanctioned by the government. In Katowice, before the advent of democracy, these tools were used by NGOs with variable effect. Now they continue to be channeled through NGOs as well—the difference being that access to official decision making is more effective with new opportunities for participation, and with many former NGO members in positions of power. In São Paulo, with a relatively new democratic structure, protests are not a regular part of civic life, though individual complaints about environmental violations have become an important source of information for enforcement agencies; promotion occurs through neighborhood associations, squatter groups, the media, and NGOs. Little information or evidence is available on the role of promotion and protest in Singrauli, Tianjin, or Tunis.

A3.52   **Coordination and Decision-making. Intersectoral** coordination to manage urban environmental affairs is lacking and has become a problem in most cities for different reasons; it works best in Jakarta and Tianjin. In Accra, there is no coordinating agency for environmental issues at the local level and, at the national level, the Environmental Protection Council has not been able to coordinate between sectors to gather data or implement policy. At the level of urban environmental services, the degree of cooperation varies department by department; there are no incentives for joint work on intersectoral matters. In Katowice and São Paulo, rational resource management and environmental planning are hampered by a lack of intersectoral coordination. This has been blamed on a lack of formal links between institutions in different sectors; for example, there are no coordinating mechanisms for water and waste management in the voivodeship. In Tunis, the urban region has special legal status and coordination should be between governorates but, in reality, decisions often involve or are made by national-level actors. Unlike the other cities, coordinating mechanisms have been established for urban development in Jakarta for both planning and implementation: (a) at the central government level, there is a planning body that is charged with synchronizing interdepartmental coordination for urban activities; (b) at the Jabotabek level, there is a committee to coordinate sectoral programs and projects from three World Bank loans; and (c) for implementation of infrastructure activities, there is a program to coordinate investments and institutional strengthening (IUIDP). Progress in cooperative management still needs to be made in the coordination of river basin management, pollution control, SWM, and local planning decisions. In Tianjin, the Urban-Rural Construction Committee is responsible for planning and implementing all urban infrastructure; to do so, it coordinates all relevant municipal bureaus, including the one responsible for environmental protection.

A3.53   Coordination **across levels of government** is improving in the more centralized systems but is problematic in the recently decentralized polities. In Ghana and India, there is an ongoing attempt to move from a top-down flow of information to a two-way movement that would allow for the expression of more local input in the formulation of development plans. In Indonesia, the mechanisms that have facilitated intersectoral coordination have brought different levels of government together. This has been especially true for infrastructure and services provided through IUIDP and the Kampung Improvement Program for low-income neighborhoods. Tianjin's special provincial status and favorable political connections have facilitated intergovernmental coordination. In Poland, initiatives began in 1992 to decentralize environmental decision making in the upper Silesian industrial region; the shift from central to local management has been hampered because the voivodeship and municipal governments have inadequate revenues. Problems of coordination across levels of government in Tunisia have been mentioned above. In the São Paulo metropolitan region, intergovernmental coordination has been stymied in some important areas because portions of some environmental services (flood prevention, sewerage, and mass transportation) are provided at different levels. For example, there are three cities in the region in which sewage collection is a municipal responsibility but treatment is the domain of the state; in these cases, the municipalities are not treating the sewage and are not connected to the state system. SWM is a municipal responsibility, but some cities do not have unregulated land available for disposal sites. However, the "not-in-my-backyard" attitude has prevailed to prevent cooperative disposal arrangements between cities.

A3.54   In the area of environmental **decision-making** and implementation, formal mechanisms for public participation are lacking in most of the cities (with the exception of São Paulo), though the need for new arrangements has been recognized in some cases. In Accra, formal participation has been limited to professionals with an interest in environmental matters or business representatives. However, subcommittees on the environment are being established by the District (local government) Assemblies to allow for more grassroots involvement. In Jakarta, there is a forum at the *kelurahan* level where community representatives can discuss problems and define development objectives. At higher levels, there are increasing numbers of consultations and workshops that involve the city and local councils with social and political groups, as well as professional associations. Formal mechanisms for public involvement in the design and implementation of environmental interventions are not yet well developed in Poland; more responsive government officials are seeking means of promoting popular participation, and NGOs are filling the gap for the time being. In Tunis, municipal commissions are supposed to represent public interests; they have a consultative role with the regional councils. In Singrauli and Tianjin, there are no formal mechanisms for popular participation in environmental decision making. With the return to democracy, several participatory mechanisms have been developing in São Paulo: (a) there is scope for public involvement in the environmental impact assessment process; (b) a state council on the environment exists where community representatives and environmental groups can participate in making decisions about environmental projects; (c) NGOs exist to express the views of interest groups on urban environmental matters; and (d) public expression is frequently voiced through the media. São Paulo is probably ahead of the other cities in terms of participation because it has had the lengthiest recent experience with democratization.

A3.55   Several of the cities have had successful experiences with **involving the private sector** in environmental management (primarily in SWM). The Accra metropolitan authority uses private contractors to collect solid and human waste from different parts of the city and makes use of private consultants for EIAs, analysis of potential dump sites, urban coastal zone management, and environmental monitoring. In Jakarta, private firms are heavily involved in toll road development and the preparation of EIAs; private sector involvement in solid waste handling, water treatment, waste treatment, and environmental education is currently being negotiated. São Paulo has completely privatized its street sweeping, solid waste collection, and disposal operations, as well as collection of industrial and commercial wastes. In Katowice, with increasing privatization and a growing number of joint ventures, there will be a need to find mechanisms for enforcing environmental management in the private sector and involving it in planning and decision making. On the negative side, powerful private sector residential, commercial, and industrial developers are often able to influence public sector agencies for their own interests.

Constraints and opportunities

A3.56   Some of the limitations on effective environmental management that have been observed in the different cities are:

- Inadequate enforcement of environmental laws, regulations, and standards (all);

- Insufficient human resources to manage environmental issues (Accra, Jakarta);

- Inconsistent rules and strategies between levels of government (Jakarta, São Paulo);

- Failure to include economic measures in the choice of tools (all);

- Macroeconomic and pricing distortions that are environmentally unsound (Katowice, Singrauli, Tianjin);

- Undue industrial sector influence in environmental decision making (Jakarta, Katowice, Singrauli);

- Poor intersectoral coordination (Accra, Katowice, São Paulo, Tunis);

- Poor intergovernmental coordination (Katowice, São Paulo, Singrauli, Tunis); and

- Failure to involve the public in decision making (Accra, Katowice, Singrauli, Tianjin, Tunis).

To a certain degree, these problems are present in all of the cities. The cases listed are where the limitation is most severe.

A3.57   To address some of these constraints, each of the cities is undertaking several initiatives to improve environmental management. Accra is focusing on planning and regulation, with the development of a national environmental action plan, transport and coastal zone planning, flood modelling, and implementation of an EIA process. Jakarta is improving its institutional capacity by creating a city-level environment agency, conducting various environmental studies, implementing integrated water basin management, providing for more NGO input in the next kampung improvement project, and strengthening institutions for pollution control, hazardous waste management, and water supply. The Katowice voivodeship is receiving technical assistance for environmental management and is developing strategies for environmental protection, waste management reform, and industrial restructuring. Activities are being initiated in the São Paulo metropolitan region to strengthen municipal institutions, manage the Guarapiranga water catchment area, and provide management assistance for sanitation and water supply, industrial pollution control, environmental health, drainage, air pollution control, and river cleanup. Three initiatives are under way for the Singrauli region: (a) coal field environmental management plans; (b) a regional environmental impact assessment; and (c) the TCPO strategic action plan. In Tianjin, urban environmental management is being improved through implementation of the 1991–1995 Urban Construction Plan (investments in water quality, drainage, transportation, district heating, and coal gasification) and a World Bank-financed project that supports several environmental investments as well as capacity building for better planning and management. The key activities in Tunis are an accelerated industrial pollution control program and several World Bank-supported infrastructure and transport projects.

Summary: Factors Affecting the Urban Environment

A3.58   To summarize this comparative analysis of the cities, a simple matrix is presented in Table A3.2 to group problem areas with their effects, causes, and managerial remedies. Information was primarily derived from the case study cities on problems, impacts, causes, and managerial responses (or the lack thereof). In general, cities will have different degrees of each problem, causes and effects will vary, and management options will be constrained in different ways (absence or presence of political will, financial and human resources, administrative and legislative rules). For example, cross-cutting causes underlying several environmental issues include: substandard housing, disease-carrying insects and rodents, and stress. The net effect of cumulative and related environmental problems is that the residents of cities have a lowered quality of life. At an aggregate level, this is manifested in health problems, reduced urban productivity, and amenity losses from degraded environmental systems.

A3.59   This summary of environmental problems, their levels of impact, causes, and effects can be misleading. The issues and options are not discrete; environmental problems are often intertwined, as are their causes. Consequently, the framework for urban environmental management, suggested in the first chapter, is needed because it considers the interrelationships between not only problems but solutions as well.

TABLE A3.2. Summary of urban environmental issues and options

Problem Area	Effects	Causes	Management Options
AIR-RELATED PROBLEMS			
AMBIENT AIR POLLUTION • community • city wide • regional • transnational	○ health problems ○ economic costs from health care costs and productivity losses ○ amenity losses (aesthetic, cultural, and recreational)	- industrialization - increase in motorized fleet & congestion - use of highly polluting fuels (leaded gas and high sulfur coal) - energy pricing policies - topography and climate	+ fuel pricing + regulations, standards, emissions charges + demand management + transport planning + appropriate technology (clean fuels, scrubbers, etc.)
INDOOR AIR POLLUTION • household • workplace	○ health problems (chronic obstructed lung disease, acute respiratory infections, low birth weights, cancer) ○ economic costs from health care & productivity losses	- use of low-quality fuels for cooking and heating (biomass and high sulfur coal) - poorly ventilated dwellings & workplaces - passive smoking - cottage industry activities	+ substitute fuel and equipment pricing + fuel switching + building codes + public education + tax hazardous products and processes
WATER-RELATED PROBLEMS			
SURFACE WATER POLLUTION • community • city wide • regional	○ health problems ○ economic costs (additional treatment, new sources of supply, health costs) ○ amenity losses	- pricing policies - unclear property rights - poor regulations and/or enforcement - municipal & industrial waste disposal practices - urban runoff - irrigation practices	+ marginal cost pricing + regulations, standards, licensing, charges + improve monitoring and enforcement + demand management and wastewater re-use + appropriate technology + land use controls + waste management
GROUNDWATER POLLUTION AND DEPLETION • community • city wide • regional	○ reduced water quality from saline intrusion, biochemical seepage ○ health impacts ○ economic costs (damage from land subsidence, health costs, increasing marginal costs of supply)	- pricing policies - unclear property rights - poor regulations and/or enforcement - unsustainable extraction - sanitation, municipal & industrial waste disposal practices - poor demand management	+ marginal cost pricing (sustainable extraction, aquifer recharge costs) + regulations, standards, licensing, charges + waste management + appropriate technology + demand management + controls on land use and sources of contamination
COASTAL/LAKE POLLUTION • community • city wide • regional • transnational	○ health effects due to contaminated seafood and direct contact ○ loss of recreational resources & tourism revenues ○ damage to fisheries ○ amenity losses ○ eutrophication	- unclear property rights - poor regulations and/or enforcement - municipal and industrial waste disposal practices - disposal of shipboard wastes	+ regulations, standards, licensing, charges + appropriate technology + coastal zone management and preservation + shipping facilities + waste management + land use controls

TABLE A3.2 (continued) Summary of urban environmental issues and options

Problem Area	Effects	Causes	Management Options
		LAND-RELATED PROBLEMS	
DEGRADATION OF LAND • city wide • periurban • regional	○ declining agricultural productivity ○ reduced renewable resource base (deforestation, lost soil fertility) ○ erosion and siltation ○ amenity losses ○ loss of natural habitat & species	- changes in relative value of land uses - uncontrolled urban growth - unclear property rights - woodfuel and land pricing - mining and quarrying activities - land disposal of municipal and industrial wastes	+ internalize ecological value in land prices + designate special areas for management + local participation + clarify property rights + economic resource pricing + land use controls
LOSS OF CULTURAL AND HISTORICAL PROPERTY • community • city wide	○ loss of heritage ○ loss of tourism revenues ○ damage to culturally valued buildings, monuments, natural sites	- land prices do not reflect social valuation - lack of regulation and/or enforcement - air pollution - SWM practices - land subsidence and poor drainage	+ internalize costs of loss in redevelopment planning + tax incentives for preservation + zone and building codes + pollution control + public education
DEGRADATION OF ECOSYSTEMS • regional	○ health hazards ○ resettlement costs ○ loss of habitat and species ○ air, water, land pollution	- failure to anticipate effects in planning and development - pricing policies - lack of rural political power	+ internalize costs of rural degradation + resource pricing + clarify property rights
		CROSS-MEDIA PROBLEMS	
MUNICIPAL SOLID WASTES • household • community • city wide • regional	○ health impacts ○ costs related to blocked drainage and flooding ○ water pollution from leachates ○ air pollution from burning ○ amenity losses	- poor management (improper collection and disposal, little resource recovery) - pricing (no cost recovery) - disposal impacts external to community - input pricing	+ private sector delivery of collection and disposal + waste minimization (recycling, recovery, source reduction) + regulations, standards, licensing, charges + expanded coverage + inst. strengthening
HAZARDOUS WASTES • household • community • city wide • regional	○ surface, ground, coastal water contamination ○ related health, economic, and resource impacts ○ accumulation of toxics in the food chain ○ reduced property values	- inadequate regulations and/or enforcement - no incentives for treatment - input pricing for waste-producing industries - low visibility, nonlinear, long-term effects - dispersed small-scale & cottage industries	+ regulations, standards, licensing, and charges + improve monitoring and enforcement + treatment and disposal incentives + economic input pricing + waste minimization + marginal cost pricing + special incentives for small-scale generators + privatization of treatment and disposal operations

continued on next page

TABLE A3.2 (continued) Summary of urban environmental issues and options

Problem Area	Effects	Causes	Management Options
NATURAL AND MAN-MADE HAZARDS • household • community • city wide • regional	° health effects (deaths, injuries) ° economic costs (loss of lives, property, infra-structure) ° land degradation (flooding, landslides, earthquakes) ° amenity losses	- natural forces - land markets failures (lack of alternatives for squatters, artificially constrained supply) - land policies (no taxation, no/unenforced protection of high-risk lands) - poor construction practices	+ reduce constraints on supply of usable land + appropriate incentives (prices, taxes, tenure, housing finance) + land use controls + improve knowledge about risks and alternatives
INADEQUATE SANITATION • household • community • city wide	° health impacts (diarrheal diseases, parasites, high infant mortality, malnutrition) ° related economic costs ° eutrophication ° amenity losses	- inappropriate technology - pricing (no cost recovery) - poor management (lack of operations and maintenance, uncoordinated investments) - inadequate hygiene education	+ gear sanitation options to willingness to pay + community approaches + cost recovery (pay for O & M, new investments) + hygiene education
INADEQUATE DRAINAGE • community • city wide	° health effects ° property damage ° accidents ° reduced urban produc-tivity (shutdown of business, transport systems)	- inadequate hygiene education - increased urban runoff due to impermeabilization and upstream deforestation - occupation of low-lying lands	+ community manage-ment of maintenance + strategic investment in drainage + land use controls & market liberalization + solid waste management

Adapted from *Towards Environmental Strategies for Cities*, UMP Discussion Paper (forthcoming), Washington, DC: World Bank, 1993, and urban environmental profiles.

REFERENCES

Bartone, Carl, J. Bernstein, and J. Leitmann. 1993. *Towards Environmental Strategies for Cities: Policy Considerations for Urban Environmental Management in Developing Countries. UMP Discussion Paper* (forthcoming). Washington, DC: World Bank.

Bartone, Carl, M. Belil, G. Karl, and A. Serra. 1990. *Technical Working Group on Urban Environmental Indicators: Final Report.* Barcelona.

Beatty, Kathleen. 1991. "Public Opinion Data for Environmental Decision Making: The Case of Colorado Springs." *Environmental Impact Assessment Review* No. 11.

Benavides, Livia. 1992. *Hazardous Waste Management for Small-scale and Cottage Industries in Developing Countries: Overview Paper.* Washington, DC: UMP.

Blore, Ian. 1993. *Guide to the Rapid Analysis of Development in Cities—RADIC (draft).* Birmingham: University of Birmingham.

S. Boyden, S. Millar, K. Newcombe, and B. O'Neill. 1981. *The Ecology of a City and Its People: The Xase of Hong Kong.* Canberra: Australian National University Press.

Chambers, Robert. 1980. *Rapid Rural Appraisal: Rationale and Repertoire. IDS Discussion Paper No. 155.* Sussex: Institute for Development Studies.

Davos, Climis, et al. 1991. "Public Priorities for Evaluating Air Quality Management Measures." *Journal of Environmental Management* No. 33.

Dunlop, Riley, G. Gallup, and A. Gallup. 1993. "International Public Opinion Toward the Environment." *Impact Assessment* Vol. 11, No. 1.

Egunjobi, Layi. 1989. "Perception of Urban Environmental Problems: A Pilot Study of the City of Ibadan, Nigeria." *African Urban Quarterly* Vol. 4, Nos. 1 & 2.

Environmental Management Associates. 1991. *Urban Environmental Priorities in Accra: Towards a Strategy for Action.* Toronto: Centre for Urban and Community Studies, University of Toronto.

de Oliveira, Jose Pedro, and C.N. Engracia de Oliveira. 1991. *Urban Environmental Priorities in São Paulo: Towards a Strategy for Action.* Toronto: Centre for Urban and Community Studies, University of Toronto.

Ford Foundation. 1993. "Urban Research in the Developing World." Reports from the Final Meetings, Cairo: Social Research Centre, American University in Cairo.

GTZ. 1993. *Manual for Urban Environmental Management.* Eschborn, Germany: GTZ.

Hadiwinoto, Suhadi. 1991. The Consultation Process and Environmental Priorities in Jakarta," in *Five Cities Meeting Briefing Document.* Toronto: Centre for Urban and Community Studies, University of Toronto.

Leitmann, Josef. 1992. "Rapid Urban Environmental Assessment: A First Step Towards Environmental Management in Cities of the Developing World." Paper presented to the 12th Annual Meeting, International Association for Impact Assessment, Washington, DC.

Lichter, Robert, and D. Amundsen. 1992. *Solid Waste Management: Comparing Expert Opinion, Media Coverage and Public Opinion.* Washington, DC: Center for Media and Public Affairs.

Linares, Carlos, D. Seligman, and D. Tunstall. 1993. *Developing Urban Environmental Indicators in Third World Cities.* Washington, DC: World Resources Institute and USAID Office of Housing and Urban Programs.

McCarney, Patricia. 1991. *Draft Terms of Reference for Local Consultants Working on "World Cities and Environment: A Five City Consultation Process."* Toronto: Centre for Urban and Community Studies, University of Toronto.

National Environment Secretariat (Kenya), Egerton University, Clark University, and World Resources Institute. 1990. *Participatory Rural Appraisal Handbook.* Washington, DC: World Resources Institute.

Population Crisis Committee. 1990. *Cities: Life in the World's 100 Largest Metropolitan Areas.* Washington, DC: Population Crisis Committee.

Schmidt, Zdzislaw. 1991. *Urban Environmental Priorities in Katowice, Poland.* Toronto: Centre for Urban and Community Studies, University of Toronto.

UN Population Fund. 1988. *Cities: Statistical, Administrative and Graphical Information on the Major Urban Areas of the World.* Barcelona: Institut d'Estudis Metropolitans de Barcelona.

USAID and US EPA. 1990. *Ranking Environmental Health Risks in Bangkok, Thailand.* Washington, DC: USAID Office of Housing and Urban Programs.

World Bank. 1992. *World Development Report 1992: Development and the Environment.* New York: Oxford University Press.

Distributors of World Bank Publications

ARGENTINA
Carlos Hirsch, SRL
Galeria Guemes
Florida 165, 4th Floor-Ofc. 453/465
1333 Buenos Aires

AUSTRALIA, PAPUA NEW GUINEA,
FIJI, SOLOMON ISLANDS,
VANUATU, AND WESTERN SAMOA
D.A. Information Services
648 Whitehorse Road
Mitcham 3132
Victoria

AUSTRIA
Gerold and Co.
Graben 31
A-1011 Wien

BANGLADESH
Micro Industries Development
    Assistance Society (MIDAS)
House 5, Road 16
Dhanmondi R/Area
Dhaka 1209

Branch offices:
Pine View, 1st Floor
100 Agrabad Commercial Area
Chittagong 4100

BELGIUM
Jean De Lannoy
Av. du Roi 202
1060 Brussels

CANADA
Le Diffuseur
151A Boul. de Mortagne
Boucherville, Québec
J4B 5E6

Renouf Publishing Co.
1294 Algoma Road
Ottawa, Ontario
K1B 3W8

CHILE
Invertec IGT S.A.
Av. Santa Maria 6400
Edificio INTEC, Of. 201
Santiago

CHINA
China Financial & Economic
    Publishing House
8, Da Fo Si Dong Jie
Beijing

COLOMBIA
Infoenlace Ltda.
Apartado Aereo 34270
Bogota D.E.

COTE D'IVOIRE
Centre d'Edition et de Diffusion
    Africaines (CEDA)
04 B.P. 541
Abidjan 04 Plateau

CYPRUS
Center of Applied Research
Cyprus College
6, Diogenes Street, Engomi
P.O. Box 2006
Nicosia

DENMARK
SamfundsLitteratur
Rosenoerns Allé 11
DK-1970 Frederiksberg C

DOMINICAN REPUBLIC
Editora Taller, C. por A.
Restauración e Isabel la Católica 309
Apartado de Correos 2190 Z-1
Santo Domingo

EGYPT, ARAB REPUBLIC OF
Al Ahram
Al Galaa Street
Cairo

The Middle East Observer
41, Sherif Street
Cairo

FINLAND
Akateeminen Kirjakauppa
P.O. Box 128
SF-00101 Helsinki 10

FRANCE
World Bank Publications
66, avenue d'Iéna
75116 Paris

GERMANY
UNO-Verlag
Poppelsdorfer Allee 55
D-5300 Bonn 1

HONG KONG, MACAO
Asia 2000 Ltd.
46-48 Wyndham Street
Winning Centre
2nd Floor
Central Hong Kong

HUNGARY
Foundation for Market Economy
Dombovari Ut 17-19
H-1117 Budapest

INDIA
Allied Publishers Private Ltd.
751 Mount Road
Madras - 600 002

Branch offices:
15 J.N. Heredia Marg
Ballard Estate
Bombay - 400 038

13/14 Asaf Ali Road
New Delhi - 110 002

17 Chittaranjan Avenue
Calcutta - 700 072

Jayadeva Hostel Building
5th Main Road, Gandhinagar
Bangalore - 560 009

3-5-1129 Kachiguda
    Cross Road
Hyderabad - 500 027

Prarthana Flats, 2nd Floor
Near Thakore Baug, Navrangpura
Ahmedabad - 380 009

Patiala House
16-A Ashok Marg
Lucknow - 226 001

Central Bazaar Road
60 Bajaj Nagar
Nagpur 440 010

INDONESIA
Pt. Indira Limited
Jalan Borobudur 20
P.O. Box 181
Jakarta 10320

IRAN
Kowkab Publishers
P.O. Box 19575-511
Tehran

IRELAND
Government Supplies Agency
4-5 Harcourt Road
Dublin 2

ISRAEL
Yozmot Literature Ltd.
P.O. Box 56055
Tel Aviv 61560

ITALY
Licosa Commissionaria Sansoni SPA
Via Duca Di Calabria, 1/1
Casella Postale 552
50125 Firenze

JAPAN
Eastern Book Service
Hongo 3-Chome, Bunkyo-ku 113
Tokyo

KENYA
Africa Book Service (E.A.) Ltd.
Quaran House, Mfangano Street
P.O. Box 45245
Nairobi

KOREA, REPUBLIC OF
Pan Korea Book Corporation
P.O. Box 101, Kwangwhamun
Seoul

Korean Stock Book Centre
P.O. Box 34
Yeoeido
Seoul

MALAYSIA
University of Malaya Cooperative
    Bookshop, Limited
P.O. Box 1127, Jalan Pantai Baru
59700 Kuala Lumpur

MEXICO
INFOTEC
Apartado Postal 22-860
14060 Tlalpan, Mexico D.F.

NETHERLANDS
De Lindeboom/InOr-Publikaties
P.O. Box 202
7480 AE Haaksbergen

NEW ZEALAND
EBSCO NZ Ltd.
Private Mail Bag 99914
New Market
Auckland

NIGERIA
University Press Limited
Three Crowns Building Jericho
Private Mail Bag 5095
Ibadan

NORWAY
Narvesen Information Center
Book Department
P.O. Box 6125 Etterstad
N-0602 Oslo 6

PAKISTAN
Mirza Book Agency
65, Shahrah-e-Quaid-e-Azam
P.O. Box No. 729
Lahore 54000

PERU
Editorial Desarrollo SA
Apartado 3824
Lima 1

PHILIPPINES
International Book Center
Suite 1703, Cityland 10
Condominium Tower 1
Ayala Avenue, H.V. dela
    Costa Extension
Makati, Metro Manila

POLAND
International Publishing Service
Ul. Piekna 31/37
00-677 Warzawa

For subscription orders:
IPS Journals
Ul. Okrezna 3
02-916 Warszawa

PORTUGAL
Livraria Portugal
Rua Do Carmo 70-74
1200 Lisbon

SAUDI ARABIA, QATAR
Jarir Book Store
P.O. Box 3196
Riyadh 11471

SINGAPORE, TAIWAN,
MYANMAR,BRUNEI
Gower Asia Pacific Pte Ltd.
Golden Wheel Building
41, Kallang Pudding, #04-03
Singapore 1334

SOUTH AFRICA, BOTSWANA
For single titles:
Oxford University Press
    Southern Africa
P.O. Box 1141
Cape Town 8000

For subscription orders:
International Subscription Service
P.O. Box 41095
Craighall
Johannesburg 2024

SPAIN
Mundi-Prensa Libros, S.A.
Castello 37
28001 Madrid

Librería Internacional AEDOS
Consell de Cent, 391
08009 Barcelona

SRI LANKA AND THE MALDIVES
Lake House Bookshop
P.O. Box 244
100, Sir Chittampalam A.
    Gardiner Mawatha
Colombo 2

SWEDEN
For single titles:
Fritzes Fackboksforetaget
Regeringsgatan 12, Box 16356
S-103 27 Stockholm

For subscription orders:
Wennergren-Williams AB
P. O. Box 1305
S-171 25 Solna

SWITZERLAND
For single titles:
Librairie Payot
Case postale 3212
CH 1002 Lausanne

For subscription orders:
Librairie Payot
Service des Abonnements
Case postale 3312
CH 1002 Lausanne

THAILAND
Central Department Store
306 Silom Road
Bangkok

TRINIDAD & TOBAGO, ANTIGUA
BARBUDA, BARBADOS,
DOMINICA, GRENADA, GUYANA,
JAMAICA, MONTSERRAT, ST.
KITTS & NEVIS, ST. LUCIA,
ST. VINCENT & GRENADINES
Systematics Studies Unit
#9 Watts Street
Curepe
Trinidad, West Indies

UNITED KINGDOM
Microinfo Ltd.
P.O. Box 3
Alton, Hampshire GU34 2PG
England